Serious Mountain Biking

Serious Mountain Biking

ANN TROMBLEY

HUMAN
KINETICS

Library of Congress Cataloging-in-Publication Data

Trombley, Ann, 1963-
  Serious mountain biking / Ann Trombley.
    p. cm.
  Includes bibliographical references and index.
  ISBN 0-7360-5499-5 (soft cover)
1. All terrain cycling. I. Title.
  GV1056.T76 2005
  796.6'3—dc22

                              2005003398

ISBN: 0-7360-5499-5

Managing Editor: Wendy McLaughlin; **Assistant Editor:** Kim Thoren; **Copyeditor:** Joanna Hatzopoulos-Portman; **Proofreader:** Anne Rogers; **Indexer:** Betty Frizzéll; **Permission Manager**: Carly Breeding; **Graphic Designer:** Nancy Rasmus; **Photo Manager:** Dan Wendt; **Cover Designer:** Keith Blomberg; **Photographer (cover):** Rob Karman; **Photographer (interior):** Rob Karman, unless otherwise noted; **Printer:** Sheridan Books.

Human Kinetics books are available at special discounts for bulk purchase. Special editions or book excerpts can also be created to specification. For details, contact the Special Sales Manager at Human Kinetics.

Printed in the United States of America   10 9 8 7 6 5 4 3 2 1

Human Kinetics
Web site: www.HumanKinetics.com

United States: Human Kinetics
P.O. Box 5076
Champaign, IL 61825-5076
800-747-4457
e-mail: humank@hkusa.com

Canada: Human Kinetics
475 Devonshire Road Unit 100
Windsor, ON N8Y 2L5
800-465-7301 (in Canada only)
e-mail: orders@hkcanada.com

Europe: Human Kinetics
107 Bradford Road
Stanningley
Leeds LS28 6AT, United Kingdom
+44 (0) 113 255 5665
e-mail: hk@hkeurope.com

Australia: Human Kinetics
57A Price Avenue
Lower Mitcham, South Australia 5062
08 8277 1555
e-mail: liaw@hkaustralia.com

New Zealand: Human Kinetics
Division of Sports Distributors NZ Ltd.
P.O. Box 300 226 Albany
North Shore City
Auckland
0064 9 448 1207
e-mail: blairc@hknewz.com

To my mother, Joan Trombley, for all your support

With love, Ann

CONTENTS

PART I
Keeping the Rubber Side Down

FOREWORD

To be a great racer you have to do two things: have fun and know the tricks of the trade to get you around the trail as quickly as possible. *Serious Mountain Biking* will give you a head start on both.

I met Ann Trombley in January of 2000 when I was 18 years old and just beginning life as a mountain bike racer with the U23 national team program. Ann was trying out for the ultimate goal of her career, the 2000 Olympic team. I was young and impressionable, and it was exciting to be surrounded by the great athletes of my sport as they prepared for the pinnacle of their careers. Ann stood out as someone who was very serious about her training and preparation, yet she still managed to enjoy herself and take time to help others. She had an amazing capacity to break down training and riding skills into components so that others could easily understand them. In my development as a cyclist, I had always been very casual and relaxed and maybe not a serious as I should have been. Ann showed me that I could be happy and easygoing yet still put on a serious game face when the time came for training or competition. This was an invaluable lesson for me and one that I apply to my life on a daily basis and have my current success to show for.

Ann made the 2000 Olympic team and competed in Sydney, where she came in 16th. I was thrilled to see her achieve her ultimate goal and experience the personal satisfaction that comes with it. Throughout the whole process she managed to keep things fun, light, and under control, even when they were anything but.

Although "retired" from full-time competition, Ann has stayed very close to the sport. You can ask any of the current pros in her hometown of Boulder, Colorado, how "retired" she is after she's ridden them into the ground on a so-called fun training ride. She'll still go out whenever the mood strikes and coach a group of riders through interval sessions by showing them firsthand just how hard to ride. These days it's not all about riding fast, though: Ann is also involved in coaching, clinics, and junior development in the cycling community. Ann presents her knowledge in a way that's easy for everyone to understand—from the newbie to the seasoned pro—and she makes you have fun while you're doing it!

In *Serious Mountain Biking* you'll learn how to carve turns, climb grunts, run baby heads, and maneuver down hills without crashing. The drills give you a chance to get out on the trail and practice on your own with the right technique to build your skills. Detailed photographs show exactly how to position your body and your bike no matter what the terrain. Pay close attention to her tips for planning and riding a race—they will help keep worries down and stamina up!

I wish Ann had written this book five years ago. I'm still learning things from her today. Enjoy the ride! See you out there.

Adam Craig

PREFACE

I am writing this book around my experiences and those of the athletes I coach. However, I learn something new from everyone I ride with as well as every race I attend. There is always room for improvement and this is not an exact science. This book is meant to give you a starting point on your way to attaining your mountain biking goals.

Mountain biking is not something that can be mastered in a year or two. It takes several years to develop the strength, endurance, balance, and coordination to become a skilled rider. You also must be prepared to shed blood, sweat, and tears! I began mountain biking around 1983-84, when a friend of mine, Phil Desrosiers, recruited friends and family to pitch in and buy me a mountain bike for my birthday. I had been riding my mother's huge ten-speed to school, and Phil thought I would be a natural on the dirt. Over the years, Phil proceeded to hammer me on the trails of Mount Tamalpias in marvelous Marin County, California. I will never forget his coaxing me to ride up Fish Gulch, which is a steep fire road climb. We got about three-quarters of the way up before I exploded into tears, bawling, "I can't ride this!" That fire road is now one of my favorite shortcuts to the top of Tam.

Riding mountain bikes and competing in races are two totally different challenges. But once you have done your first mountain bike race, I guarantee you will be hooked. What could be better than being outside and seeing the most beautiful places in your state, country, or the world, while being able to hang out with a great group of people? But in order to really enjoy the race, you have to have the skills to keep your skin and your mind intact!

The purpose of writing this book is to share my experience and tips for the intermediate to advanced mountain biker on everything from climbing grunts and riding drop-offs to planning your workouts and preparing for race day. Pro riders Susan Haywood, Adam Craig, and Alison Dunlap (just to name a few!) will guide you with special tips that work for them. Riding is an individual experience, so go at your own pace and find out what works for you.

ACKNOWLEDGMENTS

Thanks to my family for all of their love and support along the way—my mother, who propelled me forward with her positive energy, never let me give up and was always there to help; my sister, who made sure I got sleep the night before the race no matter what and cooked some awesome meals; and my brother, who did everything from telling the announcers what I made for breakfast, to running to every section of the course before I got there, and to being the life of the after-race celebration.

Also, thanks to Popsie, Grandma Jenny, Roger, Cheri, Kathy, Spencer, Peyton, and Adelyne for being there for me every step of the way. Without you all, I couldn't have made my goals.

A special thanks goes to my longtime friend and supporter Phil Desrosiers. He got me on my first mountain bike and stayed with me through the blood, sweat, and tears. I would also like to thank Stan Vinet for dragging me to my first race and traveling around Colorado in search of racing experiences. Thanks to Bob Fourney for supporting me throughout my racing career: Although he hated to pack my bike, he was always there to ride with me in questionable weather and push me to continue when the racing and traveling got tough. Thanks also to Othon Kesend for helping me gain the mental fortitude.

I would also like to thank my editors, Jennifer Walker and Wendy McLaughlin, for staying positive and pushing me forward when I felt like giving up.

Thanks go out to Adam Craig, Heather Szabo, Kerry Barnholt, Heather Irminger, Melissa Thomas, Travis Brown, Susan Haywood, Alison Dunlap, and Jeremy Horgan-Korbelski for taking the time to write down their thoughts and give up some of their secrets. And to Kevin Rice, Chloe Forsman, Mike Koenig, Heather Szabo, and Alec Uitti for being such beautiful models, and to my photographer Rob Karman for making time to shoot even in 35 degree weather! You all are the bomb!

CREDITS

Chapter 1, page 15: Adapted, by permission, from G. LeMond and K. Gordis, 1987, *Greg LeMond's complete book of bicycling* (New York: G.P. Putnam's Sons)

Chapter 1, page 16: Adapted from *Clinics in sports medicine*, V13, JC Holmes, AL Pruitt, NJ Whalen, "Lower extremity overuse in bicycling," pages 187-203, © 1994, with permission from Elsevier.

Chapter 2, page 29 (table 2.1): Adapted, by permission, from USA Cycling, Inc., 1995, *Expert level coaching manual* (Colorado Springs, CO: USA Cycling), 40.

Chapter 8, pages 129-136: Adapted, by permission, from USA Cycling, Inc., 1995, *Expert level coaching manual* (Colorado Springs, CO: USA Cycling), 123.

Chapter 9, page 140 (table 9.1): Adapted, by permission, from USA Cycling, Inc., 1995, *Expert level coaching manual* (Colorado Springs, CO: USA Cycling), 76.

Chapter 9, page 141 (table 9.2): Reprinted, by permission, from USA Cycling, Inc., *Training manual for mountain biking* (Colorado Springs, CO: USA Cycling), 6-7.

PART I

Keeping the Rubber Side Down

ONE

Choosing and Fitting Your Equipment

© Tom Moran /STPHOTO.com

For optimal efficiency and minimal risk of stress-related injury while on your bike, you need to ride a bike that is appropriate for your prevalent riding style and you need to fit correctly on it. Depending on your strengths and weaknesses, you may want to make changes to your current bike or make some decisions about buying a future one. Although most readers may already own a bike, this section is a quick rundown of the various bikes that are available for cross-country mountain biking.

SELECTING YOUR STYLE

Mountain bike racing is technically challenging and physically demanding, not just on the rider but also on the bike. An accurately fit and well-performing bike can maximize your strengths while a malfitting bike can slow your progress. Like their riders, cross-country bikes come in many shapes and sizes and have their own strengths and weaknesses. To be a good rider, you need to work at all aspects of riding to be proficient at every skill and you need to be physically fit to face challenges. Applying the same criteria to your bike, you need to select a strong bike that will enhance your performance in every skill. A good all-around cross-country mountain bike racer should be proficient at long, sustained climbs, power climbs, technical descents, and flat sections. Table 1.1 shows the relationship between these four riding styles, the strengths of riders who specialize in each style, and the type of bike needed for optimal performance.

Table 1.1   Right Bike for the Right Style

Style	Strengths	Bike
Straight climbing	Excels at riding long, sustained climbs of 5 min or more	Bike with a long top tube
Power climber	Strong at riding courses with rolling or short climbs of 30 s to 5 min	Bike with a moderate top tube length
Downhill riding	Able to bomb down courses with long, technical downhill sections	Dual-suspension bike with a short top tube and more upright riding position
Short-track specialist	Powerful; able to push big gears	Hard-tail bike that is as light as possible

If your strength is climbing, you may want to position your bike so that you are more stretched out and have a lower center of gravity, which helps to keep balance and traction on both tires. Choosing a bike with a longer top tube will ensure a lower center of gravity. Most climbers choose a lighter-weight bike as opposed to one that is heavier but more forgiving on the rough sections. Currently, aluminum frames appear to be the lightest available, although carbon fiber is also a good lightweight material. When deciding between full suspension and front suspension, keep in mind that the full-suspension bikes will be a little heavier but they are quickly catching up with the hard tail bikes on becoming lightweight. Also, rear suspension helps to keep the rear tire in contact with the ground, providing more traction. It would benefit you in climbing as long as the weight of the bike didn't slow you down. Figures 1.1 and 1.2 show the various parts of the mountain bike.

If downhill is your strength, you shouldn't worry as much about the weight of the bike as about the flexibility of the material. Titanium or steel frames are the most flexible and give you a smoother ride. Full suspension is the way to go for ripping downhills. Downhill specialists tend to sit more upright, making a shorter top tube and upright bars more favorable.

If power riding is your strength, you are better at short, rolling hills. You may want to find a bike that is between the downhill and climbing models. You should still find a fairly light bike that has some suspension but also

Figure 1.1   Parts of a mountain bike.

Rear shock

Disc brake

Figure 1.2 Drivetrain and components.

puts you in a fairly upright position. When doing short steep climbs with rolling down hills, there is not as much need to be stretched out as you would for a long climb. You would be better off sitting more upright to open up your hips and put more force through the pedals.

If you excel on courses that have sustained flat sections or if you are a short-track specialist, your best choice is a lightweight bike that is fairly stiff and responsive. A lighter bike that is more rigid will help with sustained speed on the flat sections and quickness when cornering. This type of bike allows for sustained speed and quickness when cornering.

Although I have broken up riders into four categories or riding styles, most riders have a combination of strengths and varying technical abilities. These styles and abilities can be enhanced not only with the appropriate bike and bike fit but also with the best components.

Frame Materials

Currently the most popular frame materials are steel, aluminum, titanium, and carbon fiber. This section provides basic information about these four materials so that you will know how to select the right one for you. Keep in mind that although each material has different properties, you can modify the less desirable qualities to customize a particular material to your needs. For example, you can change the diameter or thickness of the tubing walls. You can also butt the tubing, which means make the wall thick at the ends and thin in the middle, to change the quality of the ride. For the most part, with mountain bikes, we are looking to make them as light as possible but able to take a pounding and be forgiving to the rider. With this said, the thinner you can make the tubing, the lighter the bike will be. By butting the tubing, you can also make a lighter bike while keeping the stress points stronger. Much of the stress put on the frame are at the weld points. If you have a thicker tube at those points, you will have a stronger frame.

• Steel. Steel has been used as a frame material the longest. It is the heaviest and also one of the most durable frame materials. It is a fairly rigid material that is durable or stands up over several years of riding. Bikes made with steel frames also tend to be less expensive than those made of any of the other materials. My experience with steel frames is that they are a bit heavier but are more forgiving on the down hills than say aluminum. They are fairly responsive through the corners and on the climbs meaning when you begin pedaling the bike moves forward rapidly.

• Aluminum. Aluminum is one of the more popular frame materials. It is one of the lightest, second to carbon fiber, and these frames tend to be less expensive than carbon fiber and titanium. In my experience, aluminum frames are super light but are very rigid and you feel every bump and rock you hit. These are great bikes for climbing but when descending on a technical trail, you really need to pick a line and stay away from the rocks or your body will be fatigued by the time you begin climbing again. If you decide to buy an aluminum frame, I suggest you go with full suspension. That way you will have a light frame that is also forgiving on the rough sections of trail.

• Titanium. In my opinion, titanium is currently the best frame material for mountain bikes. It is moderately light, is very durable, and is forgiving or slightly flexible, yielding a smooth ride. The downside to this material is the cost. This metal is difficult to obtain. It is also more difficult to weld and work with, thus making it more expensive. If you can afford a titanium bike, it will not be the lightest but it will give you a smooth ride and the frame will last you forever.

• Carbon fiber. Carbon fiber is the newest material on the block. It is made of sheets of carbon atoms that are laid out long and thin to resemble fibers. Carbon fiber is currently the lightest material used for bike frames. Carbon fiber makes a great, light frame that also has some flexibility or is forgiving in the bumps however it's not always very durable. I have seen carbon fiber bar ends tear when you crash on them. For lighter riders, this is not as much of a problem, but the heavier you are the faster the material will break down. Carbon fiber is also not the most responsive material. If you pedal out of a corner, it will take more time for the bike to propel forward than an aluminum frame bicycle.

Now that you know the basics about these four materials, go out and ride some bikes and make your own judgments about their performance. Most bike shops will let you test ride their bikes, especially if you are planning on buying. I think it is important for you as a potential buyer to ride a number of different bikes as they all have a slightly different feel because of the frame geometry, meaning tube angles, and material. Once you have ridden 3-5 different bikes, you will begin to feel the difference in how each one rides. This will then help you to determine what feels right for you.

Drivetrain

The drivetrain is made up of the derailleur, shifters, cables, brakes, and chain—some of the most important parts on your bike (see figure 1.2). If your drivetrain isn't running smoothly, you may as well get off your bike and push.

Try not to skimp on your drivetrain. The least expensive components will break down quickly or come out of adjustment easily. You don't have to purchase the high-end components; usually, the manufacturer's second best ones are just as good. They may not be as light as those at the top of the line, but they may be more durable for less money.

You will need to choose between grip and trigger shifters. It is a matter of preference, so you should try both methods to see which one you like. Each has its advantages: Grip shifting allows you to put a bit more weight behind your shifting without having to move your fingers off of the grips while trigger shifters require a lighter touch in order to shift the gears. Trigger shifters are still the most popular, although many people like using grip shifters. I have even known a few odd souls who use the grip shifting for one derailleur and trigger shifting for the other! To each their own; it is a personal choice.

Two other parts you must be aware of include derailleurs and brakes. The derailleurs are those parts on your bike that shift the chain on to the different gears, one in the front to shift onto the different chain rings, and one on the rear to shift onto the different-sized cogs. These are both very important parts and shouldn't be scrimped on. If your bike isn't shifting well, you will not be a happy racer. For example, Shimano makes at least four different levels of drive train. The XTR is the highest level and is the lightest and responds quickly when you shift. The next level is XT, which is a bit heavier but also responds rapidly when you shift. When you are looking at components for your bike, I would suggest you get the first or second level models when buying your derailleurs—they can make or brake your race or ride.

There are two different styles of brakes that are used for mountain bikes; V-brakes and disc brakes. V-brakes use a V-style clamp that attaches to brake pads. When you pull the brake levers, the brake pads come in contact with your rim to stop you. Disc brakes are more complicated. They can be hydraulic, like motorcycle brakes, or use an air system to stop you. When you pull the brake level, the system then creates pressure on two small calipers, which clamp down on the disc.

The main differences between the two systems are weight and quickness in braking, not to mention adjustability on the fly. V-brakes are lighter but do not brake as fast or as smoothly as the disc. With disc brakes, you don't have to put as much pressure on the lever to stop you and they stop you much more rapidly. Disc brakes are much more finicky though and can be very hard to adjust especially while out on the trail while V-brakes can be adjusted in minutes. Another important difference for racers is mud clearance. V-brakes can get clogged with mud while disc brakes stay clear in muddy conditions.

If you want more in-depth detail about bikes, bike material, and components, I suggest you read books by bike-parts guru Lenard Zinn. Bike components change often. You may buy a derailleur that is top of the line, and six months later there is a new one that is even better. For up-to-date information, check out the bike magazines.

Tires

After having chosen what they feel is the perfect tire, riders often use the same tire for all conditions. This may not be a bad idea if you are continuously riding on the same terrain. However, once you begin to ride different conditions, you need different tread. The best way to discover what works best for your riding or racing conditions is to actually experience riding with different tires. If you get the chance, ride a section of a trail on one type of tire and then switch tires and ride that same section. Try a different tire on the front than on the rear; it may be your best selection.

In general, muddy conditions require tread that has small lugs, spaced far apart. Wide spacing allows for the mud to clear through the tread without building up, while still getting some traction. (Lugs, for those of you who are not familiar with the jargon, are the knobs on the tires.) Hard-pack conditions, when the dirt is a little wet or tacky, are best for high-speed riding. In these conditions, a semislick tire is best. These tires have small lugs on the outer portion with little if any tread on the middle portion, allowing for less rolling resistance and therefore higher speeds. Although the rear tire is best as a semislick tire, you may want to put a little beefier tire on the front. The front is the control tire, so you should make sure it has more traction. For example, the racecourse may contain hard-packed climbs that require less pronounced lugs to get good traction. The downhill section may have become loose and dusty from riders braking. A semislick front tire will most likely wash out or slide out on the front. Washing out on the front tire has more potential to launch you off your bike than washing out on the rear tire.

Loose-dirt or dusty conditions require both a front and a rear tire with good traction, meaning it's taller and has a more profuse number of lugs. Also, lowering the air pressure can help with traction. (Lowering the air pressure flattens the tire, giving it more contact with the ground, lessening the chance that it will slide out.) However, any time you deflate your tires, you run the risk of a pinch. A pinch flat occurs when the tire and the tube are compressed in such a way that the tube doubles up on itself and pinches, creating a hole in the tube and consequently a flat tire. This point is where the tubeless tire comes in: A tubeless tire allows you to ride with less air and therefore gives more traction without the worry about getting a flat.

Terrain that involves wet roots is the most challenging to ride on. The best tires to run in this situation have short lugs with little space between them. As in the previous discussion, you can lower the air pressure to allow for better contact with the terrain. You can pinch flat on the roots so don't take out too much air. Again, tubeless tires are always a good alternative. In rocky conditions, such as in an endless field of rocks ranging from fist size to the size of a baby's head, it is best to pump up the volume. Here again, the best tire is one with small lugs with a moderate amount of space between them. You need more air pressure to eliminate the possibility of a pinch flat when hitting the rocks. The tubeless tire should come in handy in this situation as well, because being able to decrease the air pressure will allow for a smoother ride. (See the discussion on tackling rocks in chapter 10.)

Riding on sand is similar to riding on loose dirt. It requires higher-profile lugs with less space between them. I have ridden on tires with paddle-shaped lugs that span the entire tire width. This configuration gives you the ability to paddle through the sand as a paddleboat in water. Again, low pressure is best.

Most trails and racecourses have mixed conditions. They can go from loose dirt to rocky and even wet and rooty terrain. The best tire is one that allows for good traction in every condition. When deciding what section of the course to focus on for tire selection, look at the length of each section and determine where you could lose the most time. For example, if the course is a 5-mile loop that has three or four loose, dusty downhill sections ranging from 25 feet to a quarter mile long, with the remainder of the course being hard packed, focus on the hard pack. You probably won't lose time on the loose sections, but you can definitely make up time on the hard pack. Again, try different tires so you can get a feel for what works best in various conditions.

Mountain biking on the road can be a good training tool, especially if you don't have a road bike. In this case you need to ride on slick tires or tires that have few to no knobs. Also, a tire with a smaller diameter will give you less resistance on the pavement, allowing you to go faster.

Given the preceding information on appropriate tire selection, you would benefit by bringing two or three types of tires to each race. Changing weather conditions from one day to the next will have an effect on the course. For example, it may have been hard packed while preriding but then the night before the race, it rained all night. You will then be racing on wet, muddy terrain. The course conditions can also change when a multitude of riders and racers are riding on it. The course in Mammoth Mountain, California, is generally hard packed. After three days of several hundred racers practicing and racing on the course it becomes dusty and loose, especially on the downhill sections. Be prepared!

Pedals

A variety of pedals are on the market with new ones coming out every year. When purchasing pedals, consider how easily you can get in and out of them. Other considerations are platform, mud clearance, adjustability, and float. When discussing racing pedals, I am strictly referring to the clipless kind. They mechanically attach your riding shoes to your pedals, allowing you to have constant contact with the pedals. More important, you have the ability to use the upstroke to help propel you forward. With platform pedals or ones with toe clips that go over your shoe, you only get power on the downstroke. When attached to your pedal, you have the benefit of also creating power for forward momentum on the upstroke, helping to smooth out your pedal stroke. As a result, you will be more efficient any time you are pedaling through various terrains, such as loose climbs.

If you are new to clipless pedals on your mountain bike, you can count on taking at least three months to feel comfortable with them. With clipless pedals, you cannot simply lift your foot off of the pedal; in most cases you need to twist your heel outward to detach. It takes time to learn how to get in and out of these pedals before it becomes automatic. Consequently, you should start off with a brand that is either adjustable or easy to get out of; otherwise, you will be spending quite a bit of time falling down while still attached to your pedals.

To make pedals lighter, manufacturers are making them less substantial, which means the pedal has less platform. Less platform is okay if you have a shoe with a ridged sole to help ensure all of your force is going through to the pedal. If you have less platform on the pedal and a flexible-soled shoe, a portion of your energy will be wasted.

Mud clearance is key, especially if you live where the conditions are quite muddy. Also, if you will be doing any cyclo-cross riding or racing for training, which is a style of riding and racing where you are required to get on and off your bike, a pedal with good mud clearance is imperative. A simple way to determine whether the pedal provides good mud clearance is to look at the clip and pedal interface. If there is minimal space between the clip or shoe attachment and where the clip fits on to the pedal, there will not be much room for the clip to move. Once mud clogs up on the pedal, you won't be able to get the clip out. The best way to determine weather you have good mud clearance it to try it or ask your local bike shop.

Finally, you should have some float in your pedals but not an excessive amount. Float is the ability to—or how much you can—move your heel in and out while attached to your pedal. A few years back the big thing was to get pedals with a good amount of float to take the stress off the knees. This concept is true to some extent but when you start to get too much float, the hamstrings have to work very hard to control the float. I would say being able to move your heel 1 centimeter to the left and 1 centimeter to the right from where your heel is comfortable is enough. Any more float and you will end up unnecessarily working your muscles, possibly causing muscle strain.

Full Suspension, Hard Tail, or Soft Tail

Currently some question still exists as to which bike is most efficient on a cross-country course: the fully suspended bike or the hard tail bike. The advantage of a hard tail bike is that it is lightweight for faster climbing. The disadvantage is that you take more of a beating on the downhill, which then tires you out more quickly. A full suspension bike makes going downhill faster and less stressful. And you have increased traction of the rear tire while climbing because the rear tire has more contact with the ground. The disadvantage here is that the increased weight makes it slower on the climbs and the increased bobbing while pedaling transfers to less forward momentum. A soft tail has the advantage of a small amount of rear suspension maintains the lightweight bike while decreasing the pounding on the climbs and descents. However, it does not have enough suspension to smooth out tough technical sections.

A light hard tail bike weighs 21 to 22 pounds, while a full-suspension bike will weigh between 24 and 30 pounds. All of this weight difference depends on the components you choose. The front shock can weigh from about 3 to more than 5 pounds depending on the brand, model, and amount of travel. (Travel is the distance of movement in the shock.) The travel can be anywhere from 80 to 140 millimeters. For a cross-country bike, it is more important to keep it light than to have more travel; therefore, I would stick with a shock that has 80 to 100 millimeters of travel in the front. The rear shock has anywhere from 1-3 inches of travel and weighs around half a pound. The newer shocks come with a built-in lockout mechanism. Some of them actually have the lockouts attached to the bars, so you don't have to reach down to your suspension to make the change. Locking out the shock makes it rigid or eliminates the suspension, stopping the bike from bobbing while riding uphill or on flat sections and allowing for more forward momentum. A rear shock, called "the Brain," will actually engage when you encounter bumps and become rigid when no suspension is needed.

FINDING YOUR FIT

Along with purchasing a bike that suits your racing style, you need to fit your bike to your body. When I began mountain biking, the idea of fitting your bike to your body did not exist. Of course you had to find a bike that fit your basic body size, but that was as finely tuned as you got. Now, several levels of bike fits exist. Bike fits are done to find the optimal position for power, speed, and wind resistance as well as to help minimize injury. These methods don't necessarily coincide. You can get a general fit from your local bike shop or you can go to a sports medicine clinic or specialist to get a medical bike fit. This section provides ways to do your own bike fit by using tools you most likely have around the house. It also gives you a little insight into what is done with bike fitting in a sports medicine clinic as well as some physical problems that can occur with improper positioning.

Frame Size

All frame builders are *not* alike. Currently, the sizes go from small to medium to large and extra large. This is obviously saying nothing about actual measurements. I don't find too many problems with this method of measuring because frames can be measured in several ways. Some manufacturers measure from the center of the bottom bracket to the top of the seat tube; others measure from the center of the bottom bracket to the juncture of the seat tube and top tube; and still others measure to the top of the top tube. Because the frames all have different angles, lengths of top tubes, and bends in the top tubes, it would be difficult to compare measurements anyway. A basic way to find out whether the frame is the correct size for you is to stand over the top tube in your cycling shoes and make sure you have 3 inches in between your crotch and the top tube. Another method is to ensure that only 4 to 5 inches of seat post is showing once you properly fit on the bike. Finally, if you want to use some math, a formula for fitting the frame is inseam length minus 14 inches. For instance, if you have a 32-inch inseam, the math would be 32 – 14 = 18-inch frame. But don't get too picky!

Saddle Height

You can determine appropriate saddle height using several methods. As with most of these measurements, they have been determined using a road bike. Until scientific studies are done specifically for the mountain bike, I can only go by what has been done with road bikes and tweak it slightly.

The first and simplest method of measuring saddle height is to put your bike on a trainer and do some pedaling. Once you have sufficiently warmed up, enough to feel you are in your normal riding position, unclip or take your feet out of the cages and put your heels on the pedals. While doing this, your heels should be able to stay in contact with the pedals with out your hips rocking. Move your saddle to the appropriate height until this is true.

A second method for measuring seat height is to put your cycling shoes on and stand on a fairly hard surface with your feet about 2 inches apart. Get a book or broomstick and place it in a horizontal position firmly between your legs. Measure the distance between the floor and your crotch (the top of the object between your legs). Take this measurement and multiply it by 1.09 to get the distance from the center of the pedal spindle, with the crank arm in line with top tube, to the top of the saddle.

A third method, which is recommended by Greg LeMond, is to take the same floor-to-crotch measurement as in the prior model and multiply by 0.883. Transfer this measurement to the distance from the center of the bottom bracket to the top of the saddle along the seat tube. This measurement will work out to be somewhat lower than the previous one.

Last but definitely not least is the measurement done by Holmes, Pruitt, and Whalen. They were the first people to do a scientific study on appropriate bike fitting. This is a more scientific measurement that requires a goniometer (a device for measuring angles). When measuring with this method, find someone who is competent in using a goniometer. With your bike on a trainer, do some pedaling with resistance to get your appropriate position. Then have the person line up the fulcrum of the goniometer at the rotational axis of your knee. One end of the goniometer should be pointing at your greater trochanter (the prominent bone at the hip joint) while the other end should be lined up with your lateral malleolus (the bony prominence at the outside of your ankle). This is done with the crank arm in line with the seat tube. The angle should be between 25 and 30 degrees. The angle can change if your heel position changes. Make sure you are measuring with the heel in the same position as when you are pedaling. See figure 1.3.

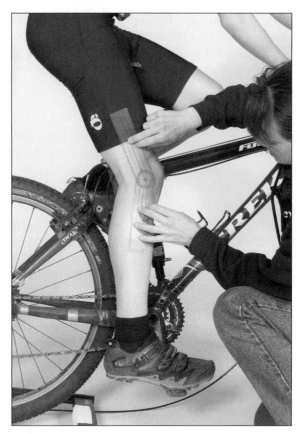

Figure 1.3 A goniometer can show you the proper angle for fitting saddle height.

If you are having any chronic aches or pains, and especially if you have any repetitive motion injuries, it is best to go to a health care practitioner who can appropriately assess your problem and give you a medical bike fit. As a physical therapist with knowledge of bike fitting and as a person who has experienced a number of stress injuries, I am biased about who is competent to fit you on your bike. In order to get a medical bike fit, I would suggest you contact either your local bike shop or physical therapy clinic. Ask them if there is someone in your area who will fit your bike in a way that will help prevent or eliminate current injuries. Another way would be to contact a cycling coach in your area, which may best be done by looking them up on the internet. USA Cycling has a list of coaches on their Web site.

Stem Length and Height

Like all of these measurements, stem length and height differ for everyone depending on comfort, body type, flexibility, and age, just to mention a few. In general, stem length should be such that when your hands
are resting on the bars, you should have a slight bend in the elbows.
You can also look at LeMond's recommendation, which is to have 1 or
2 inches between the knee and elbow when at their closest position
during the pedal stoke. One of the measurement methods used in road
cycling is to get on your bike and position yourself with your hands on
the bars and look down the trail or road and drop a plumb line from
your nose; it should bisect your bars. Also, in this same position, if
you look down at your bars, you should not be able to see your front
hub because it is directly in line with your bars. This method doesn't
work for mountain biking. My experience shows the front hub on a
mountain bike to be just behind the bar, or closer to the body, when
looking down at the bar.

You should have approximately 60 percent of your body weight on the
rear wheel and 40 percent on the front wheel while seated and on flat
ground. Here's how to measure the weight distribution: Put your front
and rear wheel on two separate bathroom scales as shown in the photo
on page 18. Find a flat surface in your house or garage that is close to
a wall. Put two scales down, one under your front tire and one under
your rear (see figure 1.4). Get on your bike with your bike gear on and
rest your hand against the wall for balance. Look at the weight on the
front scale and the rear scale, or get a friend or neighbor to do this so
you don't fall off your bike. Add the total weight of both scales and then
calculate 40 and 60 percent of that weight. For instance, if the front scale
reads 60 lbs and the rear reads 100, the total weight of bike and body
is 160 lbs. If this is the case, then you are close to perfect because 60
percent of 160 is 96 lbs, which should be the weight on the rear wheel,
and 40 percent is 64 lbs, which should be the weight on the front tires.
Don't get too specific with this; it is O.K. to be off by 5-8 percent. If your
total bike and body weight are 160 lbs, your margin of error would be
8-13 lbs. This is simply meant to be one more tool to help get you into a
good position on your bike. You should be in a position that gives you
some breathing space without having too much of your body over the
front wheel. If you have any tingling in your hands or a pain in your neck,
get those bars up higher.

Figure 1.4 Standard bathroom scales can be a great, inexpensive way to measure weight distribution.

Crank Arm Length

Crank arm length will depend on your leg length, and more specifically your femur (thigh) length. In general, mountain bikers have longer cranks than roadies. Crank arm length determines the size of the circles that you pedal and influences the leverage and RPMs you produce. Larger crank arms enable you to push bigger gears at lower RPMs and smaller crank arms help you push smaller gears at higher RPMs. Another consideration for mountain bikers is the height of the bottom bracket and therefore how much clearance you will have when your crank arm is closest to the ground.

You can determine crank arm length by your height using table 1.2. These measurements are a place to start but they are not set in stone. It is really about preference, so try different crank arm lengths to see what will give you the smoothest pedal stroke without interfering with your ability to clear objects on the trail. I am about 5 feet, 3 inches tall and I ride a 172.5 crank arm. Anything smaller and I feel I am making baby circles!

Table 1.2   Standard Crank Arm Lengths

Height	Measurement
5' and under	160mm
5'0" – 5'5"	165-172.5mm
5'5" – 6'0"	170-175mm
6'0" – 6'2"	172.5-180mm
6'2" – 6'4"	175-180 and up
6'4" and above	180mm

Saddle Position

The standard technique for measuring fore-aft position, or where the saddle sits in relation to the seat tube, is to drop a plumb line or straight edge, such as a ruler or a level, from your knee to your pedal spindle. Put your bike on a trainer and pedal for several minutes. After you are correctly positioned on your bike, put your cranks in a horizontal position in relation to the ground and drop the plumb line or straight edge from your kneecap straight down. It should fall directly in front of the pedal spindle (see figure 1.5). When measuring, make sure your heel remains in the same position as when you are pedaling. Moving the heel up or down can drastically change where the plumb line falls.

Be aware that the saddle position can determine what muscles are most used. With the saddle more fore, a cyclist tends to use primarily the quadriceps and with the saddle more aft the gluteal muscles. The more fore position can also put a lot of stress on the kneecap. So, if you have chronic knee pain, do not put your saddle in this position.

As for saddle tilt, or whether your saddle is nose up or nose down, most riders should position their saddles to be level. You can do so by putting a level on your saddle, or you can eyeball it. If you have numbness or unnecessary pressure, play with the position or get fit by a professional.

Choosing a comfortable saddle can be very difficult. Everyone has a different anatomy. The main weight-bearing bones are the ischial tuberosities, also called sit bones because they are under the gluteal muscles that you sit on. The saddle should be wide enough to support these bones to avoid the pain of sitting on soft tissue. Generally, women have wider hips than men and therefore need to find a saddle that is wider at the base or tail end of the saddle while men can tolerate a narrow base. It is a good idea for both sexes to have a saddle that is concave or has a dip or hole between the base and the nose. This space takes

Figure 1.5   By dropping a plumb line from your knee you can accurately measure the fore-aft position.

the pressure off of the soft tissue or genitalia and distributes it between the ischial tuberosities, which is where it should be.

The only way to truly determine whether a saddle is right for you is to go for a ride. If you are lucky, a bike shop will allow you to try out different saddles. Once you have found a saddle that fits you well, I suggest you buy at least two of them. You never know when they will go out of production and you will have to go through the whole process again. What a pain in the rear!

Bars

The standard rule for bar width is to keep it equal to your shoulder width. Measure the shoulders from one acromioclavicular joint, or bony prominence on top or your shoulder, to the other. The measurement you get for your shoulder width should be the same for your bar width.

An argument for narrowing the bars on a bike is to allow access through close obstacles, namely trees and boulders. The 2000 Olympic course in Sydney had a section where you had to thread yourself and your bike between a boulder and a tree. When fresh, or while preriding the course, the obstacle was easy to clear. However, during the last lap of the race I hit the tree, which knocked me into the boulder and stopped me in my tracks as well as tore my cool saddle. As a result, I lost at least one position in the race. A few months later, I heard that Paola Pezzo, the Olympic champion, had narrowed her bars to fit through the obstacles on the course. Every ride is a learning opportunity!

Whether you use bar ends is a personal preference. I like to use them because they provide a second position in which to put my hands and they put me in a better position to climb. Having your hands on the bar ends causes you to reach farther, effectively lowering your center of gravity. However, they can also get caught on trees and other cyclists if you are in close proximity. Try them and decide for yourself.

Physical Variables

Many individual physical variables can affect how you position yourself on your bike. Following are the most common ones. Having tight hamstrings can cause excess stress on the low back, especially if you are in a more aerodynamic position or your torso is more horizontal to the ground. In this case you may want to raise your bars up to take the stress off of the low back and stretch your hamstrings!

If you have relatively long legs and a short torso, you'll want to look for a frame that takes this proportion into account. So, the top tube should be shorter or you can have a shorter stem and longer crank arms. The converse is true for short legs and longer torso: Look for a frame with a longer top tube or get a longer stem and shorter crank arms.

Back pain, as just mentioned, can result from excessive flexion in the low back because of tight hamstrings. You may get increased pressure on the low back by tilting the saddle with the nose up as well. Low-back pain can result from weak trunk strength, too. You may want to try to reposition yourself on your bike, but if it doesn't work, you should consult a professional. Neck pain is generally a result of increased neck extension or having to crane your neck up. In this case you should increase the angle on your stem or change the seat-to-stem difference to put you in a more upright position.

Leg-length differences can cause various aches and pains, especially saddle sores. If you have a leg-length discrepancy, you need to determine whether it is in the femur (thigh) or tibia (calf). With femur differences, you can adjust the cleat positions, moving the cleat slightly fore on the shorter leg and slightly aft on the longer leg. With tibia differences, you may need to put a lift in between your shoe and your cleat. Again, this is something that should be done by a professional, such as a physical therapist, who is trained to look at these differences.

GETTING YOUR GEAR

Choosing appropriate riding gear is just as important as choosing a bike. Shoes, clothing, and helmets are not just accessories; they are necessities for enhancing safety and comfort, and therefore performance.

Like other shoes, bike shoes should be fit to your feet. Different brands tend to vary in width; a knowledgeable bike store assistant should be able to tell you which ones are suited for your width. Most cyclists' feet will swell slightly after 20 to 30 minutes of riding, so make sure you have enough room in the toe box. If you have any numbness or tingling in you foot or toes after riding for 20 to 30 minutes, you may need to get a wider shoe. Tingling in the toes or a sensation of heat can result from pinching the nerves between the toes. To eliminate this problem, you may want to move your cleat forward or backward on the shoe or get a metatarsal pad that sits in your shoe just below your toe joints. You may be able to find a metatarsal pad in your local drug store. Supported insoles for your shoes may also help to eliminate pressure on bony points of your feet. You can find insoles in your local drug store or a good running shoe store. The best way to get an appropriate fit is to go to a bike fit specialist. Foot pain can make or break a good ride, so don't scrimp. A good guide for bike fit and cycling related issues is Andy Pruitt's *Medical Guide for Cyclists.*

As with your saddle, once you find shorts that are comfortable, you should buy several pairs. Make sure that the shammy, or padding, is a good wicking material that covers the sit bones as well as the pubic bone. I find it best to have a thin shammy with no seams other than around the edges. Any extra stitching can cause chaffing and possible saddle sores—Ouch!

Your helmet is one of the most important pieces of equipment, don't leave home with out it! There are several different brands of helmet. Most if not all have a safety label that goes with them. You may want to check this before you purchase one. Your helmet should fit snugly without giving you a headache. Most helmets come with several different padding thicknesses to help adjust for comfort. You can also adjust the straps to ensure that the helmet is secure. When trying on a helmet, shake your head around to make sure that the helmet does not move. You also need good ventilation, which most helmets provide. Whether to have a visor is a personal preference. I like the shading effect, especially in the winter months when the sun is low, and when going in and out of trees. I think I may be considered old school!

Mountain biking encompasses many skills but in order to be your best and start off on the best foot possible, you have to have the right equipment. It's all about personal preference. Choose a bike that fits your style and works well on the terrains you will be covering. Get fitted by a professional; riding should be enjoyable, not painstaking! And choose a gear that's practical and comfortable. There's no point in racing if your equipment is more painful than the physical demands of the race.

TWO

Climbing Steep Grunts

To be a competent racer, you must master climbing. They say the race is won on the climbs, perhaps because a large percent of mountain bike race courses are held on ski slopes. This ensures that a large portion of the course will be a climb. About 40 percent of the racecourse contains uphill sections. This chapter features the techniques I know from my own experience to help you become a climbing specialist by getting physically fit, positioning yourself correctly on your bike, learning the best way to pedal uphill, and understanding how best to conserve your energy.

OFF THE WEIGHT, UP THE POWER

Climbing is about weight-strength ratio. If you are light and can push a lot of watts, you will be an exceptional climber. That said, you can still increase your climbing ability in two ways: Change the weight of your bike or your body and increase your power output.

You can lighten your bike by using lighter components, but many people go overboard in this area. I have talked with many riders who will change out bolts on their bike just to make them an ounce or two lighter. You can actually make your bike too light. A really light bike tends to bounce around a lot more, making your ride a lot less comfortable.

Decreasing your body weight is more effective than adding that titanium bolt to the seat post. I have seen pro cyclists lose a large amount of weight over the winter, then race really well that following season. This observation is not scientific proof, so don't get crazy. Taking off body weight should be done in a controlled manner and should not be done in excess; a cyclist needs enough fuel to propel the bike forward. If you think you would benefit by losing weight or would just like to change to a more healthful diet, see your doctor or make an appointment with a dietitian to determine what diet would work best for you. Proper nutrition is a huge part of riding and racing well, and can enhance your overall fitness.

Increasing watts, or power output, will improve cycling performance. To increase your power output, you need to ride above the level at which you are comfortable riding. You can do so with intervals, such as hill repeats, or by pushing yourself harder on a given section of the trail. In order to measure your progress, you can purchase a power meter, heart rate monitor or simply time yourself on various sections of a course or trail to make sure you are going faster. I will discuss in more detail the various training tools and when to test your progress in chapter 9. You can purchase a power meter to measure this function; however, power meters are too expensive for most of us, so try to find a lab near you that can test for power output. If a lab is not available, don't sweat it. Heart rate monitors are still very effective tools for cycling as is simply timing yourself on various sections of a course or trail to make sure you are going faster. I will discuss in more detail the various training tools in chapter 9.

POSITIONING FOR THE CLIMB

Good climbing requires a low center of gravity. You can lower your center of gravity by changing your body position on the bike or by making the geometry of the bike such that it positions you lower.

To redistribute your body weight on the bike, scoot your rear back on the saddle, bend your elbows, and bring your chest down. This position works well if that climb isn't too steep. Once the climbs become so steep that your front wheel begins to lift off the trail, you need to get more body weight on the front half of your bike by scooting your rear forward on the saddle, so that you are resting on the nose, while continuing to keep your elbows bent and chest down low (see figure 2.1). This skill takes time and experience to hone because each trail is different in its pitch and looseness. The more time you spend on your bike on the trails, the more comfortable you will get with this technique.

You can reposition your bike to lower your center of gravity in a number of ways. One way is to get a bike that has a slightly longer top tube, which will force your body to a more stretched position, lowering the center

© Roving Photo

Figure 2.1 Keep your weight low and even over the wheels and let your legs do the rest.

of gravity. You can also use bar ends (extenders attached at the end of your bars) to change your hand position while riding, helping to stretch your body out on the bike and get your upper body lower over the top tube. If the frame you lust for does not have a long top tube, you can also attach a longer stem, again stretching you out over the bike and getting your center of gravity low. Be aware that a longer stem also affects the way your bike handles, making it a little less responsive when turning the bars. Also, if you have back or neck pain or tight hamstrings, you have to watch that you aren't too stretched out. My advice for anyone with neck or back pain is to get a bike that provides the most comfort to you on all terrain and then make adjustments in your body positioning for the various grades of the trail.

PEDALING UPHILL

Of all types of cyclists, mountain bikers have the widest range of pedaling cadence (see table 2.1). Our cadence is both very fast and very slow; you need to be able to push a big gear when going downhill or on the flats but you need to have a fast cadence when climbing, especially on loose surfaces. To keep traction on those loose climbs, whether they contain loose dirt, rocks, or sand, you must have a smooth pedal stroke.

A choppy or uneven pedal stroke or mashing (meaning putting most of your weight on the downstroke) makes it difficult to stay upright on the steep, loose climbs. An uneven pedal stroke causes the rear tire to lose

Table 2.1   Pedaling Cadence

Discipline	RPM
Road	90-110
Individual time trial	85-100
Team time trial	85-95
Individual pursuit	100-125
Team pursuit	135+
Points race	120-150
Kilometer	125+
Sprint	140-160
Mountain biking	50-150
Cyclo-cross	60-130

STEEP CLIMBS

Jeremy Horgan-Korbelski

© Courtesy of Gary Fisher Bicycles

"The most important thing about climbing steep or technical hills is maintaining a balance between rear-wheel traction and controlling the front wheel. You do this by shifting your weight forward or backward on the bike depending on the conditions of the climb. If the ground is really loose or muddy, it's important to sit down and keep weight over your rear wheel to keep it from spinning. In those kinds of conditions it's important to emphasize a smooth, circular pedal stroke to keep your wheel from slipping out. On the other hand, when the climbing is really steep, it's important to lean over the front of the bike in order to keep weight over the handlebars to maintain control and go where you want to. The art of steep and technical climbing is finding the balance between these extremes depending on the conditions and pitch of the trail."

traction and off you come, hoping to land on your feet and not on your face. Distributing the weight as evenly as possible throughout the pedal stoke keeps the rear tire in better contact with the terrain and you spend less time working on your cyclo-cross skills. In terms of biomechanics, you don't actually fire your muscles much on the upstroke. In effect, you are actually controlling the downstroke. What ever the case may be, I can attest to the fact that smoothing out your stroke will make you a better mountain bike rider.

I have done three types of pedal stroke drills that I also have my athletes perform: single-leg drills (SLDs), high-cadence drills (HCDs), and strength and endurance intervals. Another way to improve pedal stroke is to spend some time riding a single-speed or fixed-gear bike. Also, if you or someone you know owns a CompuTrainer, it may be a good idea for you to get on it. The CompuTrainer has a function that allows you to monitor the smoothness of your pedal stroke as well as compare the efficiency of one leg to the other.

Single-Leg

Single-leg drills require pedaling with one leg at a time. Isolating each leg helps to make the pedal stroke a circular motion to strengthen each leg separately. We all have one leg that is stronger than the other and the stronger leg will do more of the work when pedaling with both legs. When you pedal with one leg, the weaker leg is forced to do as much work as the stronger leg. You also become more aware of the unevenness of your stroke. Many cyclists begin pedaling using mainly their quadriceps, an action we call mashing the gears because all the force is on the downstroke. With practice you can utilize more muscle groups while pedaling, making you a more efficient rider.

SINGLE-LEG DRILL

PURPOSE
To increase muscle strength by working various muscle groups while pedaling with one leg.

WARM-UP
Warm up for 20 minutes at an easy effort.

TECHNIQUE
Work on a trainer or flat road. Put your resting foot on the bottle cage, rear triangle or on the trainer beside you. Pedal for 30 seconds with the clipped in foot, working on making it as smooth as possible. Pedal with both feet for 1 minute before switching to the other foot.

TIPS

Concentrate on what you are doing and not trying to simply get them over with. Think about making circles, a rotating wheel, a steam train, or whatever you can that will help you to make smoother circles.

PROGRESSION

Start slowly. Begin with 4 to 5 repetitions in one session then ramp them up each week for the next 3 weeks before you go back to 4-5 intervals. Every 4-week session I usually increase the time until the rider has reached a minute for each leg. The drill schedule looks something like this:

Week 1: 1 day of SLDs at 5×30 seconds
Week 2: 1 day of SLDs at 6×30 seconds
Week 3: 1 day of SLDs at 7×30 seconds
Week 4: 1 day of SLDs at 8×30 seconds
Week 5: 1 day of SLDs at 5×45 seconds
Week 6: 1 day of SLDs at 6×45 seconds
Week 7: 1 day of SLDs at 7×45 seconds
Week 8: 1 day of SLDs at 8×45 seconds

High-Cadence

High-cadence drills are done for the same reason as the single-leg drills, but with a slightly different spin. By pedaling at a high speed with less resistance, you are forced to have a smooth pedal stroke.

HIGH-CADENCE DRILL

PURPOSE

To improve your stroke by pedaling in a smaller gear at high cadence.

WARM-UP

Warm up for 15 to 20 minutes at an easy pace.

TECHNIQUE

Once you're warmed up, get into a high or easy gear, small chain ring in the front and third from largest in the rear, and spin as fast as you can without bouncing out of the saddle. Do this exercise from 20 seconds to 1 minute before doing an easy spin for 1 to 2 minutes. Repeat 8 to 10 times in one session.

TIPS

This drill is best done on a trainer but you can also try it on rollers. Rollers will make it more challenging because it adds balance.

PROGRESSION

Start small and increase the time or number of drills as you get more proficient. After 3 weeks of ramping up you should always take an easy or taper week to recuperate.

- Week 1: 1 day of HCD's of 5 x 10 seconds, with a 2 minute EZ spin in between each. (Easy week)
- Week 2: 1 day of HCD's of 10 x 10 seconds, with a 2 minute EZ spin in between each.
- Week 3: 1 day of HCD's of 10 x 20 seconds, with a 2 minute EZ spin in between each.
- Week 4: 1 day of HCD's of 10 x 30 seconds, with a 2 minute EZ spin in between each.
- Week 5: 1 day of HCD's of 5 x 10 seconds, with a 2 minute EZ spin in between each. (Easy week)
- Week 6: 1 day of HCD's of 15 x 10 seconds, with a 2 minute EZ spin in between each.
- Week 7: 1 day of HCD's of 15 x 20 seconds, with a 2 minute EZ spin in between each.
- Week 8: 1 day of HCD's of 15 x 30 seconds, with a 2 minute EZ spin in between each.

Strength and Endurance

I have my riders do these drills after they have been on their bikes for several months or in the specialization phase II, which is discussed later in the book. This timing ensures that they have some strength in their muscles and tendons and are less likely to injure themselves while performing the drills. Strength and endurance drills are really good for helping increase you strength on short power climbs as well as for smoothing out your pedal stroke.

STRENGTH AND ENDURANCE DRILL

PURPOSE

To smooth out your pedal stroke while increasing strength in the pedal stroke.

WARM-UP

Ride at an easy pace for 15-20 minutes or for as long as it takes you to get to an appropriate hill.

TECHNIQUE

Find a hill that will take at least 5 minutes to climb. It is best if the hill isn't too steep since you need to remain in a moderately hard gear. Get into a big or hard gear, big chain ring in the front and third to smallest in the rear. Pedal uphill for 5 to 8 minutes going slowly and working on a circular pedal stroke. Then go downhill or pedal in an easy or low gear for 5 to 8 minutes before going again.

Build up your endurance by pedaling up and down a small hill keeping an even pedal stroke.

TIPS

Concentrate on a smooth pedal stroke. Visualize yourself closing the gap on a rider in front of you while keeping a smooth pedal stroke.

PROGRESSION

> Week 1: 1 day a week of SED's of 4 x 3 minutes, with a 5-minute EZ spin in between each.
>
> Week 2: 1 day a week of SED's of 5 x 3 minutes, with a 5-minute EZ spin in between each.
>
> Week 3: 1 day a week of SED's of 6 x 3 minutes, with a 5-minute EZ spin in between each.
>
> Week 4: 1 day a week of SED's of 7 x 3 minutes, with a 5-minute EZ spin in between each.
>
> Week 5: 1 day a week of SED's of 4 x 4 minutes, with a 5-minute EZ spin in between each.
>
> Week 6: 1 day a week of SED's of 5 x 4 minutes, with a 5-minute EZ spin in between each.
>
> Week 7: 1 day a week of SED's of 6 x 4 minutes, with a 5-minute EZ spin in between each.
>
> Week 8: 1 day a week of SED's of 7 x 4 minutes, with a 5-minute EZ spin in between each.

I hope you are getting the picture of the progression. I wouldn't have my athletes go much past 5 minutes at a time or 8 repetitions. After they do these for 2-3 months, it is time to change drills. You don't want to get bored!

This schedule may seem too simple and you may be tempted to make it more challenging, but try it; you will be amazed at how taxing leg drills can be. Any time you get the urge to jump ahead and ramp up more quickly, remember that it takes at least four times as long to recover from an injury than to sustain one. In other words, overtraining can keep you off your bike for months at a time.

CONSERVING YOUR ENERGY

Climbing on a mountain bike is all about energy conservation. This concept is especially true for any climb with an extremely hairy technical section or steep, loose section. When riding a trail, notice where the terrain gets tough or really difficult to climb. This area is where you need enough energy to push through. While climbing, keep a moderate pace (around lactate threshold, discussed further in Chapter 10, which is the point at which your body begins accumulating lactic acid) and a smooth pedal stroke. When you see a tough technical section coming up, back off slightly on your effort. You can do so by decreasing your heart rate by 5 to 10 beats, if you are wearing a heart rate monitor, or decreasing your effort by one number on a rate of perceived exertion (RPE) scale of 1 to 10. (See chapter 9 for discussion on RPE scales.) Once you reach the tough section, you should have enough energy to then muscle it through. Many times you need to stand or slightly lift your rear end off the saddle to get enough leverage to make it over the tough sections. This technique may also require you to go anaerobic for a short distance. Once you get through the difficult section, back off again on the intensity until you recover enough to get back to a moderate pace or lactate threshold.

A well-seasoned mountain bike rider goes through this routine when riding any type of single track or technical climb. It becomes automatic after several years of practice. One of the intervals I use to get better at this skill is the hill repeat, which is discussed in detail at the end of this chapter.

Sit or Stand

Climbing on a mountain bike can be done while in the saddle or by standing. Things that will determine whether you sit or stand while climbing are: terrain, fatigue level, and how quickly you need to close a gap between you and another rider or racer.

Unlike road cyclists, mountain bikers don't do a lot of standing on their bikes. Many conditions, especially when climbing, make standing nearly impossible. The most difficult time to climb on your bike is when the trail becomes steep and loose or, worse yet, a trail with wet roots.

Standing to pedal causes a redistribution of your weight on the bike. It shifts from a higher percentage on the rear wheel to an equal or higher percentage on the front wheel. With this change, less traction occurs on the rear wheel and the rear tire is more likely to kick out or lose traction. You can get your rear end back and shift your body weight backward to remedy this situation (see figure 2.2). This skill definitely needs practice. Basically, when riding on fire roads or hard-pack conditions, standing can be a good change of pace. If you are on a course that is loose or riddled with wet roots, sitting may be your only option.

Some mountain bikers stand on a climb simply to rest. Pedaling while seated causes the body to fire specific muscle groups, mainly the quadriceps and gluteal muscles. By standing, you can decrease the use of these muscles or change the way they are used, and use more

Figure 2.2. Shift your body weight back so that more pedal strength is generated on the front wheel.

of your body weight to help propel the bike forward. Standing isn't done without a significant amount of effort. It increases your heart rate because it causes you to use more muscles, such as your core stabilizers and upper-body muscles. However, standing for short periods can be a good method to give your body a change of pace, whether mental or physical.

Lastly, tactical maneuvering in a race may determine whether you need to sit or stand on a climb. Generally, standing can help propel you forward a lot faster than sitting because you push a harder gear for a shorter amount of time, by getting your body weight over the pedals.

If you are in a situation where you need to lose a cyclist who is on your wheel, you want to pass a cyclist before reaching a single-track section, or you just want to close the gap on a cyclist ahead of you, standing and sprinting can give you the acceleration you need. If you are not in one of these situations, sitting is the most energy efficient way to climb.

By maintaining your seat on the climb you get the most out of your energy.

SPRINT LIKE YOU MEAN IT

PURPOSE

To practice tactical maneuvering in sprint positions.

WARM-UP

Riding at an easy to moderate pace for 20 to 30 minutes.

TECHNIQUE

A mountain biking sprint generally lasts from 8 to 30 seconds and should be done while standing. Shift in to your big chain ring in the front and middle to small cogs in the back, get out of the saddle and sprint for 8-30 seconds. After each sprint, ride easy for 5 minutes.

TIPS

Keep it fun. Try sprinting with a friend or a group of riders. Any time the road funnels into a single track, sprint as hard as you can to see who makes it in to the single track first. The more similar you make these sprints to an actual race situation, the more prepared you'll be. On a road bike, you can practice by sprinting to every yellow sign or whatever sign tickles your fancy that day.

PROGRESSION

Week 1: One day a week of 5 x 15 second sprints, with a 5-minute easy spin in between each.

Week 2: One day a week of 6 x 15 second sprints, with a 5-minute easy spin in between each.

Week 3: One day a week of 7 x 15 second sprints, with a 5-minute easy spin in between each.

Week 4: One day a week of 8 x 15 second sprints, with a 5-minute easy spin in between each.

Week 5: One day a week of 5 x 20 second sprints, with a 5-minute easy spin in between each.

Week 6: One day a week of 6 x 20 second sprints, with a 5-minute easy spin in between each.

Week 7: One day a week of 7 x 20 second sprints, with a 5-minute easy spin in between each.

Week 8: One day a week of 8 x 20 second sprints, with a 5-minute easy spin in between each.

Practicing With Intervals

You need to do several intervals to increase your climbing talent. Phil Hackbarth of Total Performance Institute in Colorado Springs, Colorado, gave me my most favorite torture sessions. Since then, I have passed the hill repeat drills along to the athletes I coach.

HILL REPEATS

PURPOSE

To increase your climbing ability and strength through hill practice.

WARM-UP

Find a hill that takes 10 to 30 minutes to climb. Warm up for 20-30 at an easy pace.

TECHNIQUE

Start with 2 sets of 10-minute hill repeats. Break with a 10-minute easy spin in between each. For example: If the total interval is 10 minutes, go for 4 ½ minutes at or below lactate threshold and sprint for 30 seconds. Go back to lactate threshold for 4½ minutes and sprint for 30 seconds. Then ride at an easy pace for 10 minutes. Intervals can range from 10 to 20 minutes. Choose the increments that are most appropriate for you. Time increments can also vary from 3 minutes to 4½ minutes, making the sprint from 2 minutes to 30 seconds, respectively. Practice doing 2 to 4 repetitions of the interval (depending on the length), and remember to rest about as long as the interval time.

The most important thing to remember when setting up intervals is that they should closely resemble what you will be doing when riding or racing. If you want to gain an advantage against your competitors on the hills, these intervals will do the trick. The purpose is not only to increase your power at lactate threshold, but also to educate your body to clear the lactic acid accumulated in a sprint. In more common terms, these intervals will help increase your speed while climbing as well as give you the ability to accelerate, effectively throwing off your opponents. Remaining at the same speed will make your competitors more likely to stay on your wheel. Surprise them with a sprint out of nowhere and then go back to a moderate pace, and they will have a harder time keeping up.

The best way to test whether you are getting better at climbing is to time yourself. Pick out a climb in your area and time how long it takes you to go from the bottom to the top. After several weeks of training, time yourself again. If you are not getting up the hill faster than previous times, you may not be training properly. Time of day, wind, temperature, and when you ate last are a few factors that also may influence your time. All things being equal, after 6 to 8 weeks of training, you should be charging up that hill at breakneck speed!

THREE

Carving Turns

Cornering is all about body english or proper weight shifting, as are most of the technical skills you will perform on your mountain bike. Some other key elements in carving turns are proper braking, focus, and pedal placement. This chapter will give you some techniques for mastery in carving the perfect turn such as weight shifting, pedal placement, countersteering and braking, setting up, and cornering in challenging conditions. These techniques will not take the place of years of riding, but should give you a leg up.

WEIGHT SHIFTING THROUGH CORNERS

You must learn the technique of weight shifting to excel technically in mountain biking. Your bike does the riding while you hover over the saddle and shift your weight to control where your bike will go. I like to think of it as a dance. You are leading your bike through a series of difficult steps that become effortless with time.

When approaching a turn, you increase the weight on your front wheel. The front wheel is your drive wheel; it ensures you'll make the turn while the rear wheel just comes along for the ride. Shift your body weight from being over the base or back of the saddle, to being over the nose of the saddle either by standing and taking all of the weight off of your saddle and actually bringing your hips over the nose of your saddle, or while seated, by scooting on to the nose of the saddle and bringing your shoulders and head down closer to the bars (see figure 3.1).

Figure 3.1   By standing and leaning slightly forward you will shift weight to the front wheel.

If the turn is banked, or built up on the outside of the corner, you can simply lean in the direction of the turn and countersteer. For example, on a fire road with a banked turn to the left, put your body weight forward and slightly to the left. If the turn is off camber, or falls away on the outside, you should countersteer and shift your weight slightly to the outside of the corner or directly over your bike. Shifting your weight to the outside of the corner will help you put more pressure down through the tire, keeping traction with the dirt. For example, when taking an off-camber corner to the left, your weight should be shifted forward and slightly to the right to ensure downward pressure on the tires.

Once you come to the end of the corner, shift your weight back to the center to keep the rear wheel from sliding out. For the most part, you should have your rear just slightly off the saddle so as not to get bucked off if you hit any obstacles. With a full-suspension bike, you are more likely to absorb any obstacle, but you should still be levitating.

PEDAL PLACEMENT

Pedal placement will differ depending on the tightness of each corner. For those long, sweeping corners, or corners with berms, keep your pedals in the 12 o'clock and 6 o'clock position (see figure 3.2). This position will also effectively put more pressure through the outside of the tires helping to keep them in contact with the trail. When the corner gets tight, such as a tight switch back, you should keep your pedals in the 3 o'clock and 9 o'clock position to help keep your weight off of the saddle so you can steer more effectively. Keeping the inside pedal up, in both cornering positions, will also keep you from hitting obstacles on the inside of the corner. If the corner is extremely tight, is on loose terrain, or is off camber, taking your inside foot off of the pedal may ensure that you stay upright. (The outside pedal stays down while the inside foot is flexed back (dorsiflexed) with the knee slightly bent and leg jutting out in the directions you are going.) If the bike starts to lose traction and wash out, your inside foot will be there to catch you and pop you back up into riding position. This technique is more commonly used in down hilling or 4-cross, where platform pedals are utilized, making it easy to take your foot on and off with out clipping in or out. Use this technique cautiously as your foot can get caught in an obstacle, such as a rock or root, and get twisted or worse yet broken.

Figure 3.2   Keep the pedals in the 3 and 9 o'clock positions, flex the inside leg, and jut the bent knee in the direction you're turning.

COUNTERSTEERING AND BRAKING

Countersteering on a bike is similar to the position of the wheels as seen in race car driving. Basically, the front wheel is turned away from the direction of the turn so that you don't overcorrect or steer too much in the direction of the turn and go into a spin and crash. It's all about physics. So, if you are coming in to a right-handed corner, straighten the right arm, bending the left elbow and gently steer to the left (see figure 3.3). This movement is very subtle; if you are forcing your bike to do this maneuver, you are working too hard. Let if flow!

Figure 3.3 Turn the wheel in the opposite direction you're turning to avoid overcorrecting.

Most, if not all, of your braking should be done before you get to the corner. Once in the corner, either lightly feather the brakes or take your hands completely off the levers. Using your brakes in the apex, or middle of the corner, makes you more likely to take a digger ending up with your bike and body on the ground. Grabbing a handful of front or rear brake can cause you to lose traction and wash out. Have some confidence and let it go!

The front brake stops you faster than the rear. The weight of the bike and your body are behind the front brake, causing a more rapid deceleration while the rear brake has to drag the bike and your body to a stop. Basically more weight is on the rear brake and therefore it takes longer to stop. When approaching a turn too fast, you should shift your

CARVING TURNS

Heather Irminger

© Courtesy of Rob Karman

"When carving a turn, there are two really key things that help me execute the corner. One is simply looking ahead! I always try to look at least 10 feet in front of my front tire, all the way through the turn and where I want to end up. The second thing I think of is turning my hips so that my centerline is facing that spot that I'm looking towards. Looking ahead, squaring my hips off into the corner, and keeping a loose and relaxed upper body can turn a scary curve into a fun ride!"

rear back in the saddle and grab a little more front brake. Although it is best to use both front and rear brakes equally, in a crucial situation you should shift your weight back and utilize the power of the front brake.

When the corner is super tight and a the dirt is a little loose, you may be tempted to skid out because it will get your rear tire around the corner faster. But if you are concerned about the integrity of the trails at all, don't do it. Skidding creates huge ruts in the corners and screws up the trail. You may have to do a track stand, coming to almost a complete stop before angling your bike around the other side of a corner. When you choose not to skid, the International Mountain Bicycling Association (IMBA) and the rest of us who want to continue riding the trails will thank you for not creating any braking bumps. Sometimes, such as when you come flying into a tight turn with loose dirt, you may not be able to prevent skidding. However, skidding to try and get around a turn is not always the best method. Once you skid, your rear tire breaks loose from the terrain and it is harder to regain control. Your tire may then keep skidding and completely wash, causing you to be left in the dirt while other riders go screaming by.

SET UP AND EXECUTION

When carving a turn, always look where you want to go! When making tight switchbacks, as well as executing most difficult maneuvers on your mountain bike, you will go in the direction of your gaze. So if you look over the edge of a cliff, you can kiss your rear good-bye. With that said, when coming up on a switchback, look around to the other side and down the trail and your bike will follow. It seems a very simple concept, but it really works.

If the corner is banked or has a berm on the outside, just go to the outside and start on the top of the bank and ride it down. If the corner is off camber or tight, set up wide or as far on the outside of the trail as possible. At the apex of the corner, cut in or straighten out the turn. Then when exiting, come back to the outside or widest part of the corner. In this instance you are in effect squaring off the corner.

CORNERING IN CHALLENGING CONDITIONS

Any condition you are not used to riding in is a challenge. I have done most of my riding in northern California and Colorado. In Colorado, the trails are generally loose and rocky. California has some wet, muddy conditions, but can also be dry and hard packed. The most challenging conditions for me are wet and rooty, so let's start there.

In wet or muddy conditions your tires may already have some mud built up between the lugs, resulting in less traction. So when you come into the muddy corner, both your front and rear tire have more of a tendency to wash out. You need to come in to the corner at a slow speed to avoid having to pull your breaks when in the corner.

You also have to think ahead when coming in to the corner to avoid grabbing your brakes all at once. You need to slowly feather you brakes when coming in to the corner, then let them go once you have started to turn. Use this technique when roots are in the corner, but try to hit the roots at a right angle if possible. Never brake on wet roots!

Lastly, once you have begun cornering in wet conditions, do not shift your weight because you are more likely to slide out. It is best to keep your weight centered over your bike because any movement forward, backward, or side to side can cause you to slide out. When you come into the corner, keep your body hovering over your saddle, equally distributed over each wheel, and stay in that position while going around the corner.

Gravel and sandy conditions while cornering are similar to wet or muddy conditions. The difference is, your tires are not clogged with mud to start off with and you may have hard-pack conditions leading up to the turn. Clear tires allow for more traction leading up to the turn as well as going through it. Your brakes will respond faster and you can come in to the turn faster. For both of these conditions, it is still wise to do all of your braking before the turn and let it roll through the corner. Similarly, you shift your weight as little as possible once you are in the corner.

Loose-sweeping fire road corners can be taken at a higher speed following all of the techniques mentioned so far. The most important thing to be aware of with this type of terrain is not to pull too much front brake. Either use your brakes equally or use mostly the rear brake to ensure that you don't wash out your front tire and end up on the ground.

In any tight cornering conditions, the key is to look where you want to go and your bike will follow. You may feel the urge to put your inside foot out to give you balance, which is okay as long as you are not going too fast and no rocks or roots are in your way. You don't want to break your ankle while trying to shave off 5 seconds from your time; it's not worth it!

I can't stress enough the importance of experience in this sport, and it applies to cornering as well. You will encounter endless variations of conditions in your riding or racing. The more you practice on different terrain, the better your response will be when you encounter unfamiliar territory.

CORNERING THROUGH OBSTACLES

PURPOSE

To practice cornering skills by working through an obstacle course at different lengths and variations.

WARM-UP

Warm up 15-20 minutes at an easy pace.

TECHNIQUE

Set up an obstacle course in a parking lot or a nearby open area with dirt. Set the obstacles in a line about 5 feet apart. You can use cones, flags, rocks, stumps, or whatever debris you can find. This works best if you set the cones on a gradual decline. Start 10 feet away from the first obstacle at the top of the decline. When you come to the first obstacle, go around it to the left or right, working on shifting your weight to the outside and putting the outside pedal down. If you chose to go right around the first obstacle, go left around the next, working again on weight shifting and putting your weight on the outside pedal (see figure 3.4). Once you have done that successfully, add to those skills by going around the obstacles and bringing your weight slightly forward and to the outside. Look ahead to the next cone you will be going around.

Figure 3.4 Practice cornering by setting up obstacles and weaving tightly through them.

TIPS

When you are smoothly going around the obstacles, you should look like your bike is doing all the moving while your body stays in one position. Once you have mastered two or three skills, add in another. Don't overwhelm yourself by trying to think about too many skills at one time; practicing two or three is enough.

PROGRESSION

Once you are comfortable with the cones at 5 feet apart, move them closer together and go through them again working on the same skills. This is a good way to practice if you are not near trails that have tight corners or if the weather isn't conducive to riding the trails.

Once you feel comfortable on the obstacle course, or if you are anxious to go out on the trails, you should begin honing your cornering skills on wide fire road corners and gradually work toward the tighter switchbacks, or turns.

CORNERING ON THE TRAIL

PURPOSE

To improve your cornering skills through practice on various types of turns.

WARM-UP

Warm up with 15-20 minute ride to the trail or do some easy riding on the trail.

TECHNIQUE

Find a wide sweeping turn to the left or right, whatever side you are most comfortable turning into, and practice two skills such as putting the outside leg down, shifting your weight to the outside, feathering your brakes, looking 5 feet ahead, or carving around the corner and bringing your weight slightly forward. After you've practiced on your dominant leg, practice cornering on the side you are less comfortable with.

TIPS

Road bikes are a great tool for practicing the wide sweeping corners before getting on to your mountain bike. Start by practicing two of the skills mentioned above and add the others when you feel comfortable. Once you are comfortable going to one side, switch and practice going to the other side. Practicing all of these skills can be less scary on a road bike because you will have more traction on the road.

You may only get to two or three skills at a time and get tired of practicing. Cycling is all about having fun so just practice some of the skills and then go out and ride. You may find you want to practice more skills after you have had a chance to do some nonstructured riding, or maybe not. Don't force it.

Once you feel confident with your technique on the wide sweeping turns on a dirt road, progress to the single track tight switchbacks. For most of us, these are the hardest corners to master but can be the most rewarding once you do. If you ride or race at all, you will have to tackle a plethora of tight switchbacks and the fastest way through them is to ride, so get practicing!.

SWITCHBACKS

PURPOSE

To become proficient at riding tight single track switchbacks.

WARM-UP

Warm up by doing some bike sweeping fire road corners before doing the single track switchbacks.

TECHNIQUE

The technique for riding tight switchbacks is slightly different. Start by finding a corner that goes in the direction you are most comfortable with and then pick two skills to work on. The skills for tight switchbacks include:

1. Weight shifting slightly forward
2. Keeping your pedals level or at 3 o'clock and 9 o'clock
3. Rear off the saddle
4. Look where you want to go (see figure 3.5).

Once you have excelled at two of the skills, add another until you can go through the corner with out having to think about the technique and you are flowing like water. Once you are comfortable cornering to one side, practice the same skills going the other way.

TIPS

Remember, give yourself some time—Rome wasn't built in a day. If after three tries you aren't able to make some of the tight turns, just move on. Frustration can hinder your progress by distracting you. Accept the fact that some days you are in the groove and some days are full of ruts.

Figure 3.5 Keep a tight reign on switchbacks by shifting your weight forward and keeping your feet in proper position.

As I have mentioned, most of us feel more comfortable going either to the right or to the left when cornering on the trail. It is important to work on the side you are less comfortable with to eventually be equally competent going in both directions. If you have difficulty cornering to the right, make it a point to stop on a right-hand corner and practice.

Lastly, when trying to better any of your skills, follow someone more competent than you. By watching and mimicking how a skilled rider takes a corner, you may learn something that will help you with your technique. There is always room for improvement; don't be too cocky! As with climbing, the only way to gauge your progress on cornering is to time yourself. When you first begin your practice session, time yourself down a section of the course. After practicing several of the skills, time yourself again. You may also want to invite one of the local pros or fast downhillers out to time them on the section as well. Any amount of time you can shave off your cornering and downhilling is a good thing. If it is a long 10-minute downhill, shaving off a minute is great. If it is a 5-minute downhill, shaving 15-30 seconds is wonderful. Just look at some of the downhillers' times in their races. The time difference can be less than a second. For us cross-country types, if your race is 3 laps and you have shaved 30 seconds off your downhill time for each lap, you have decreased your race time by a minute and a half overall. That can be the difference between first and fifth place. Also, remember that running with your bike can be the quickest option.

FOUR

Flying on the Downside

Although the race is generally won on the climbs, you have to be fast on the downhill sections, too. Stay ahead of your opponents while descending, or you will give up all the time you have gained on the climbs. This chapter covers what it takes to be fast while going downhill by controlling your bike on several different types of terrain, such as loose dirt, mud, and sand, as well as the dreaded drop-off. After reading this chapter, you will know what it took me years of trial and error to learn. Don't get me wrong—you will need to practice—but I hope that your learning curve will be faster than mine was.

CONTROL ON THE DOWNHILL

One of the hardest skills in mountain biking is staying in control while flying downhill. Increasing your comfort level while descending takes years of practice, trial and error, and becoming intimate with the terrain. To get better at most techniques in this sport, you have to be prepared to crash, a common consequence of descending. As the saying goes: If you don't crash, you're not trying hard enough. Now that you have the point, let me give you some ways of decreasing the learning curve and maybe lessening the time you spend off your bike and in the dirt. The key components to becoming a fast descender are to stay loose and float above your bike, keep your weight back while riding out of the saddle, feather the brakes, and look ahead.

Floating Above Your Bike

One of the first skills I teach mountain bikers of all levels is how to use the body as a shock absorber. This also teaches you how to shift your body weight and not be afraid to take your weight off the saddle. You can use this skill any time you are off your saddle, whether it be on a flat section or while climbing a rocky or rooty technical section. However, its primary use is while going downhill. You may have a front-suspension or fully suspended bike, but that is only part of your shock absorbing ability. A big part of smoothing out the ride comes from using your joints to dampen the jarring effect of the terrain; in other words, flexing your shoulders, elbows, wrists, knees, ankles, and hips. Have you noticed that efficient downhillers look as if their trunk is not moving? In effect, they are floating above the bike. They flex and extend the joints in the limbs while letting the bike take up all of the ruggedness of the terrain. So to be an efficient downhiller, let the bike do the riding while you float on top.

Fully suspended bikes are a slightly different story. If you have chosen to forgo the weight penalty of riding a fully suspended bike or you are lucky enough to have a light full-suspension bike, you will use the previous technique less often. Fully suspended bikes allow you to sit in the saddle over much rougher terrain before having to stand. However, even full-suspension bikes are not able to take up all of the bumps of any mountain bike course and I can assure you that at some point on that downhill, you will be utilizing the floating technique.

Rising Out of the Saddle

No matter what type of bike you are on, when the pitch of the descent gets steep you will need to get your rear off the saddle. I will never forget the World Championships in Are, Sweden, for many reasons, one of which was the scary descents. Several sections in the course had a scary downhill pitch, and the course was wet and slippery. And having three or four Swiss military personnel in fatigues sitting at the top of each section with stretchers and first-aid kits definitely added to the thrill. After my first preride of the course, I thought I would definitely be running these sections. I even tried to get the military guys to show me how to ride one of the sections, on my bike that is, but they declined. By the time I had ridden the course another two or three times, I had the descents dialed, meaning I could ride them without a problem. The key was to get my rear off and behind the saddle and stay off the front brake.

Sometimes the descent is so steep, you will need to actually rest your stomach on the saddle, helping to get your center of gravity even lower while visually making you feel closer to the ground (see figure 4.1). Another technique is to clamp your thighs on to the back of the saddle while your rear is off the back, which helps you to stay in control of the rear end of the bike. In these steep situations, you are no longer steering with your bars but shifting your weight to get the bike to maneuver, so it is important to have some contact with the saddle.

One of the most important aspects to learn when going down hill is how to shift your weight in order to control the movement of your bike. This may be just getting your rear off the saddle and keeping your elbows bent to actually scooting your rear behind the saddle. Both of which will help get your center of gravity lower and allow you to steer your bike with your body. The following drill will give you some practice so you're ready come race day.

Figure 4.1   Stomaching the saddle to make the descent.

BODY ENGLISH ON THE DOWNHILL

PURPOSE
To learn control and weight shifting.

WARM-UP
Warm up for 15-20 minutes at an easy spin.

TECHNIQUE
While riding on a flat, less technical trail or fire road, practice scooting your rear off of the back of the saddle while gripping the saddle with your thighs as if you were sitting down in a chair. Once you feel comfortable on a flat section, find a slightly downhill slope and progress to a steep downhill.

Try shifting the weight of your hips gently from side to side while in the downhill position. This will give you an idea of how you can actually steer your bike by shifting your weight. When practicing weight shifting, keep your bars pointing straight ahead and move your hips from side to side.

Braking Guidelines

The best time to brake is never. Okay, it may not be an option, especially if you're on a long descent. If the descent is short and steep, brake just before you get there, and let it roll down the hill. Once you get to the flatter, more stable surface at the bottom of the pitch, apply the brakes.

When negotiating a longer descent, you should still do most of your braking before the pitch. Once you are on the downhill, you should feather the brakes, which means lightly gripping both the front and the rear brake equally so that you continue on a smooth path. It is fairly obvious that if you grab too much front brake you will most likely go over the bars. If you grab too hard on the rear brake, you will wash out the rear tire.

© Roving Photo

On steep, loose descents brake early and feather the brakes until you are in the clear.

RIDING STEEP, LOOSE DESCENTS

Kerry Barnholt

© Courtesy of Gary Fisher Bicycles

"Ride the bike as you would a surfboard, stay loose and let it move underneath you. Except, instead of hanging 10 toes off the front of the board, hang two butt cheeks off the back of the saddle."

The two hardest surfaces to negotiate on a steep descent are wet, muddy conditions and loose, dry conditions. The Mammoth, California, NORBA national event in 1999 had one such descent; it was called the No Fear Zone. One of the venues had a 50-foot drop that was basically a 5-inch thickness of dust. The technique for surviving this section was to brake before you dropped in to the powder, gently feather the brakes through the middle, and then let them go at the bottom. Without enough speed, you would get bogged down and fall over. With too much speed, the front tire would start to wobble and you would get pitched forward.

With a wet and rooty downhill, the technique again is to modulate the braking between feathering and off. When on the muddy section, it is best to do some braking to slow yourself down. When you come to a root ball, let off on the brakes completely. While in contact with the mud, the tires will have some ability to get traction and slow the bike down. Braking on wet roots will cause you to lose traction and slide out so fast that you won't know what happened. For more in-depth information on how to ride wet roots go to chapter 5.

Looking Ahead

You won't find a mathematical formula that states how far down the trail a rider should look to set up for upcoming obstacles. What you don't want to do is look directly in front of your front tire because you'll overbrake and go extremely slow. Once you have scanned the trail up ahead, your brain will remember it and make your body adjust appropriately, allowing you to increase your speed with confidence. Although you should already have some experience with this skill from walking, driving, skiing, or river rafting, it takes time to master on the bike. As a general rule, keep your eyes scanning between 5 and 10 feet down the trail at all times.

We know that the shortest distance between two points is a straight line. So why don't we always pick the straightest path when descending a trail? One reason is that obstacles encountered on the straight path, such as big rocks or stumps, may be unridable. Another, less inventive reason is that we all tend to follow the most worn path. When riding a trail, notice what line you tend to follow. In most cases it will be the one that most other people have chosen to ride and is therefore packed down. But the most common line may not actually be the fastest. When looking down the trail, use your peripheral vision to scan the width. Look for ways that you can lessen the angles of the corners or straighten out the trail. I am not telling you to go off course; it's illegal to do so in a race. It is also not in the best interest of the landscape to make drastic changes to the trail.

Within the designated trail you can generally get from point A to point B in several ways. Ideally you want to go the straightest route, but that isn't always possible so you need to time yourself to see which path proves the best. To figure out the most efficient course, use the test you use for other aspects of this sport: timing. Time yourself through each section, or have a teammate or buddy ride one line while you ride the other, to find out which path is fastest.

Descending on Full Suspension

If you are not currently riding on a full-suspension bike, borrow or rent one and try it out. Many downhill racers actually practice technical skills on motocross motorcycles. Riding a full suspension bike will have a less dramatic effect than riding a motorcycle, but it will give you an idea of how it feels to ride the same trail at a higher speed. When riding a full-suspension bike, you don't have to worry as much about picking a line. You can simply ride over obstacles that may have been daunting on your hardtail bike. Once you have gained confidence by riding the full-suspension bike, your technical skills should improve also while riding the hardtail. You should be less hesitant to take a line that may be more risky or increase your speed on the same lines you have been riding on your hardtail.

Following a Downhiller

One of the best ways to improve your downhill skills is to go out on the course with a downhill racer. I had the privilege of being on a team with Shaums March. He was an extremely fast downhiller who was also gracious enough to help out his fellow teammates. It is always a good idea to ask for help. You may be surprised how willing a downhiller is to teaching you some tricks. I had Shaums help me with a super sketchy section of the cross-country course at one of the NORBA Nationals in Vermont in 1998. I couldn't get past the drop at the top, so I was running part of the section and then trying to get back on my bike on the second half. Shaums first had me watch him while he rode the whole section. He mentioned that it was harder than what many downhillers were riding on their course. He then educated me on how to pick the section apart—ride the first gnarly part several times, then ride the second section several times. After you have confidence riding them separately, ride them both together. It worked like a charm for me.

Another technique is to ride behind a fast downhiller. By following their line, and by the simple fact that they had the guts to ride it, you may gain confidence to ride it as well. I was bombing down a trail in Nederland,

Colorado, behind Kerry Barnholt. I had never been on the trail before, so I didn't know what to expect. She came in to a technical section and rode it with no problem. Being right on her tail, I just followed her line. If I had come upon that section on my own, I probably would have wimped out. Thanks, Kerry. You're awesome.

Lastly, if you're not in the groove that day, don't push it. Some days we feel at one with our bikes and some days we don't. If you don't have the confidence at that time, just run it and move on. Hopefully you will get another chance to try it again.

THE DROP-OFF

Dropping off of a rock or tree stump is an exhilarating experience, especially if it is steeper than anything you have ridden before. The Olympic course in Sydney, Australia, had several sketchy drop-offs. One in particular was a drop off of a log that was about 3 feet down. Okay, maybe it was only 2.5 feet. Every time I rode it I would scrape my chainring and get bucked forward. Did I stress *every time* I came up to this obstacle? Sure I did, but riding it sure beat running.

Here's what you need to ask yourself to negotiate drop-offs of any kind: How steep is the drop? Can my bottom bracket or chainring clear enough that I won't get pitched forward? What follows the drop-off? And when riding a drop, the technique you need to use is this: Get your rear off and behind the saddle while effectively pushing your bike off of the drop, brake before the drop, let it roll over, and always look ahead.

Chainring Clearance

The first thing you should do when you come up to a questionable drop is measure the distance from the top to the bottom. Do so by getting off your bike and rolling it over the drop-off. No, I don't mean ghost riding (pushing your bike over the edge and letting it roll on its own). Stand at the top of the drop-off and hang on to the bike seat while letting the bike roll down (see figure 4.2). Watch to see whether the big chainring hits the lip of the drop or not. If the chainring clears, you are good to go. If, on the other hand, your chainring hits the obstacle on the lip, you either have to launch your bike over it, get your hips back so you don't get bucked off when your chainring hits, or run.

To launch it you will have to come up to the drop with some speed and do a wheelie or jump off the lip to ensure that your front chainring clears the obstacle on the top. This method is an option when no further obstacles exist below the drop and the pitch isn't too steep. However, if you see more obstacles below the drop, such as sharp rocks or wet

Figure 4.2   Checking for chainring clearance.

roots, you may choose to run. Let me tell you, I am not opposed to running.

If the obstacle at the lip of the drop is somewhat forgiving, meaning your chainring won't auger in and totally stop your forward momentum, you may still be safe to ride. The speed at which you come up to the drop can also determine whether your chainring makes it through the obstacle or not. If you are going too slow, the chances of lodging your chainring in to the obstacle are greater. Speed is your friend.

Run or Ride

As discussed in the downhill section, you may have to pick apart a technical section that has one or more drop-offs littered in between gnarly rocks or roots before deciding whether to run or ride. If the section clearly has two or three parts, pick them apart either physically or in your mind, and ride each one separately. Notice how others are riding the section or whether a less hairy line exists. If none of these techniques work, run.

Actually, it is most often faster to ride a drop-off than to run. Generally it is only a small section of the trail and it would take longer to dismount and mount than to stay on your bike. Most, if not all, drop-offs are on a downhill section. Getting off your bike while on a downhill will result in cutting off your speed. If you have practiced the section and feel confident you can ride it, don't hesitate. If, on the other hand, you have only been able to clear the obstacle 25 to 50 percent of the times you have practiced it, run it. The winner of the race is whoever *makes* it to the finish line the fastest—no matter how you get there.

Downhill Dilemmas

Ride the drop-off as you would a steep downhill section. When you come up to the lip, get your rear off and slightly behind the saddle (*a*). In effect, you are pushing your bike off of the drop. Your weight needs to be on the rear tire when you first take the drop (*b*). If you have too much weight forward when your front tire hits, your shock will compress and most likely stop, causing you to go over the bars. Once the front tire hits the dirt, you need to shift your weight to the middle of the bike. Doing so helps you avoid getting bucked off of the saddle when the back tire hits ground (*c*). See figures 4.3a-c.

Do not brake too hard at the top of the drop; you may be catapulted off the saddle when the tire hits the ground, an event I like to call the *bucking bronco effect.* It can occur when you brake too much, you don't have enough speed when you go off the drop, or you have too much weight on the saddle when your rear tire hits. It is best to lightly brake before you come to the drop and let it roll over the drop. Better yet, get your hands off the brakes until both tires are on the ground after the drop. A little extra speed is not a problem. Braking too much or engaging your front brake as you hit the ground will make the front wheel stop while you keep moving over the bars. The rear brake is a safer bet, but can still cause the bucking bronco effect when the rear tire hits the ground. In many situations in Mountain biking, staying off your brakes will create the smoothest ride, and this is one of them.

Never look directly at the bottom of the drop. As when cornering and descending, you should be looking at least 4 feet down the trail. As stated earlier, always look were you want to go to ensure that you continue the forward momentum down the trail. Looking where you want to go will give you a better chance of getting there and of setting up for the next possible obstacle in your path. If you look directly below the drop, you will most likely stop there.

a

b

c

Figure 4.3 (*a*) Entry, (*b*) drop-off, (*c*) exit.

Any time you are headed in a straight downhill path, you should keep your pedals parallel to the ground or at 3 o'clock and 9 o'clock. This position will not only give you a platform to stand on and help get your rear off the saddle, it will also ensure that you don't hit any high-profile obstacles. Keeping your pedals parallel to the ground is especially important when dropping off a ledge. Imagine that you come up to a rock drop-off and you have one pedal down. The next thing you know, your pedal is hitting the rock and once again you are thrown forward. For a woman, it means the pubic bone is in contact with the stem. For a man, I can only imagine. So, learn this lesson from this book instead of by your own painful experience.

Now that you have read through the technique of riding a drop-off, it is time to practice. The best way to get comfortable riding a drop-off is to start small. Curbs are a natural starting point. They may seem too easy but any time I teach anything, whether it be how to walk correctly after an ACL reconstruction surgery or how to ride a technical section, I have people over-emphasize the motion.

THE GNARLY DROP-OFF

PURPOSE
To build your confidence when riding technical drop-offs.

WARM-UP
Warm up with a 15-20 minute ride.

TECHNIQUE
Find a small curb in front of your house and practice riding off it. Try to find a curb that has a long section of flat pavement or grass leading up to the curb.

1. Ride up to the curb and ride off it without thinking about what you need to do (the purpose is just to get the feel). Try riding off the curb by getting your rear off and behind the saddle and pushing your bike forward.

2. Practice coming up to the curb at a higher speed, feathering the brakes just before the drop and then performing the technique as above.

3. Go out on the trail and find a log or rock drop off that isn't too daunting and practice what you have learned above. Slowly work up to that gnarly drop-off that has been plaguing you.

TIPS

Never hesitate. If you come up to the drop and stop at the lip, back up and try it again. If on the second time you don't commit, call it a day and come back another time. As with any downhill skill, it is great to follow someone who is confident. If you just stay behind them and go with the flow, you will be surprised what you can ride.

I will never forget watching some of the racers go off Bailey's Bailout on the Vail World Cup course in 1996. It was a 5-foot, rocky drop-off that landed you on a sketchy rocky section. It had to be the rush of a lifetime, especially on a hardtail! I'm not afraid to say I ran it.

Tackling Tough Terrain

© Icon Sports Media

So far in this book you have learned what it takes to be an expert at climbing, turning, and downhilling and you know how to perform these skills on the right equipment that fits your body and style. But by now you also know that the terrain you're riding is never ideal or predictable, so you have to be flexible, adapting your riding techniques as well as your equipment to fit the changing environment. This chapter will teach you how to tackle all types of terrain—wet roots, sand pits, rocks, and water—and drills for you the practice the techniques for getting through them.

WET ROOTS

As discussed in chapter 3, any unfamiliar terrain is a challenge. And, being able to ride on any given terrain requires practice on that type of terrain. Having spent most of my riding time in northern California and Colorado, both of which are relatively rocky and dry, early in my career I was not very familiar with wet roots. But later, after years of racing on the East Coast and in Europe, I got better on this terrain. Even after several years of practice, wet roots are still the hardest conditions for me to master.

Riding on wet roots requires good tires with some traction. Notice the word *some* in the previous sentence. No tire can give you full traction on wet roots, but the section on tire selection in chapter 1 will give you a few ideas. Basically, you need a tire that has shorter lugs that are spread out so you can still get traction even if you have collected a lot of mud. This arrangement ensures that the tire will clear more mud.

If you are lucky, you will have only one wet root to tackle at a time. In this case, try to angle your bike so that the front tire will hit the root at a right angle. By hitting the root at 90 degrees, your tire will have less surface area in contact with the root (see figure 5.1). Because a wet root is very slippery and does not provide much traction, it is best to get your tires back on the dirt as fast as possible. It will also keep all of your weight and the momentum of the bike going straight over the root. If you are not able to go over the root at a right angle, because of its position across the trail or because obstacles before and after the root prevent you from setting up at a right angle, again find the angle that will allow you to spend as little time on the root as possible. The more time your tires are in contact with the root, the more likely you are to slide off and crash. Get your tires back on the mud or dirt; it is less slippery.

Try to avoid pedaling when on a single wet root or cluster of them because you may not get traction, causing you to lose your balance and crash. Sometimes you will need to pedal, such as when climbing, but you

Figure 5.1 Attack wet roots at 90 degree angles to avoid slipping off and crashing.

should do it smoothly. For more information on how to climb on wet roots read the section on braking and pedaling.

Riding over one wet root is easy enough, but in general, where you see one root many will follow! When coming up to a web of wet roots, it is still best to enter at a right angle to the first root. Another detail to look for is the distance between the start and the finish of the cluster. Choosing a path within the cluster that has a smaller area will get you off those roots as quickly as possible (see figure 5.2). With that said, it is generally best to ride close to the tree that is sending out the roots. The closer to the tree you get, the more likely you are to have just one or two big roots that don't take up as much of the trail. The farther you get away from the tree, the bigger the meshwork of roots. And the fewer roots you have to maneuver over, the better for your ride.

When approaching a cluster of wet roots, you also should steer as little as possible; any jerky movements with your handlebars will cause you to lose traction. Set up the angle of entry so that you can go straight through the mangle and have a smooth exit point. I remember the Vermont National course had a downhill section with a jumble of wet roots. If you went straight, which was the easiest line with the least number of roots, you headed straight for a big mud bog at the bottom that was not ridable. Avoiding the mud bog meant you had to

Figure 5.2   Stick as close to the tree as possible and choose the root cluster with the smallest area.

start the downhill on the left side. With this line you ended up hitting a few more wet roots but you were more likely to stay out of the bog. The technique was to get over to the left side and keep your steering straight ahead, not braking as you went over the roots. If all went well, you would float over the root bed without slipping and exit on the outside of the bog. Once you were over the root bed you could start feathering your brakes and steer around the bog and on to the less muddy course. I saw many crash victims that day (myself included!), but the cheering of the crowds that gathered to watch the spectacle kept everyone laughing.

RIDING WET ROOTS

Susan Haywood

© Michael Andrick/West Virginia Division of Tourism

"Often times negotiating wet roots can be the most challenging skill to master in mountain biking. As I approach a root section, I slowly lower my speed so my reaction time increases. I maintain enough speed to keep good momentum because, as we know, momentum is our friend. As always, I think positively, believing that I can clear it successfully because what the mind conceives, the body achieves. I then assume a good body stance with my pedals at the 3 o'clock and 9 o'clock positions with my rear hovering over the saddle. I have my chin level, eyes scanning the terrain ahead. My shoulders and arms are relaxed. My fingers are staged to finesse the brakes. I lift or unweight the front wheel slightly and allow my front suspension to absorb the impacts. I then focus the rest of my body on doing the "root dance." I think of the bike as my partner and the roots as the music. I allow myself to relenquish a bit of the lead to the tempo of the roots. Of course, you try to hit the roots in a perpendicular manner, but often times you have to dance or go with the flow of the terrain. I find relaxing and being fluid out dances the sudden, stiff hurk and jerk and allows me the keep the rubber side up. The mistake I most often see made is that riders grab their brakes too strongly and too often in root sections. Also, if it is going to be a long wet day of riding roots, I ride with lower air pressure in my tires to help with traction."

Approaching Wet Terrain

As with all other skills in mountain biking, weight shifting is very important when hitting a single wet root. When your front tire is in contact with the root, shift your weight to the rear tire to effectively lift the front tire over the root. Once your front tire is over the root, shift your weight forward, allowing your rear tire to lift over the root. Imagine you are light on your bike, or floating over the root. Riders use this technique for sharp objects and the dreaded water bar, too. A water bar is a buildup in the trail that directs the water off the trail to keep it from eroding. Water bars can be made of anything from dirt to a log or an old tire. Both the log and the tire become very slippery when wet and become very difficult to pedal over, especially when going uphill.

Braking and Pedaling

Whatever you do, never grab your brakes, especially the front one, while your tires are in contact with wet roots. If you so much as tap the front brake, you will go down so fast that you won't know what hit you. Similar to when on loose and dusty conditions, you need to brake before your bike touches any wet roots. When coming up to a rooty section, lightly feather both breaks just enough that you keep a comfortable speed over the roots. Once off the roots, you can grab the brakes again. If you are lucky, the rooty sections will be on the downhill. In this case you should not have to think about pedaling. On the other hand, if wet root clusters spanning more than a foot of the trail are on the uphill, you will need to pedal. The technique for this situation is to have some momentum when your front tire hits the roots. Once you are in the thick of it, keep your pedal stroke smooth to keep the forward momentum going. A jerky stroke will cause your rear tire to slide off the root. When deciding what path to take through the root ball, take the shortest path possible. Also, pay attention to how close together the roots are. A path that is less dense has more mud or dirt between the roots, which means you get more traction. Any time your tire hits the mud or dirt between the roots, the tire will stick better, allowing you to get some traction for pedaling

Again, the course that comes to mind when talking about pedaling over wet roots is the NORBA National in Vermont, which has been in the series since around 1997. I believe it was 1998 that the promoters cut a new course through the roots and trees specifically for the race, which meant the roots were more exposed. When they cut the course it hadn't rained, so riding the dry terrain wasn't too difficult. However, for the two days leading up to the race it rained, making the fresh-cut trail very slippery and almost impossible to ride up. After we complained about the impossible riding conditions, the promoters cut out some of the uphill sections, but what was left was still no cakewalk. As I learned from my experience, the best way to ride such a course is to first stay calm; if you get anxious you tend to get more squirrelly or jittery, which can make you crash. Second, keep a smooth pedal stroke so that you can ride as much as possible before sliding off the trail. Third, don't be afraid to run. Once you get tired toward the end of the race it's really hard to keep your pedal stroke smooth and you're more likely to crash and get frustrated. In this race, running was a better option. Once I found myself slipping on the roots and crashing two or three times, it was time to get off the bike and run.

Lastly, don't ever hesitate. If you don't think you can ride the sections, you won't. In that case, plan to get off and run. When you feel confident that you can ride the roots, you will! Just think light and float right over them. Don't wait until you are on a wet and rooty course to practice your skills. Go out and find something in your area that closely resembles the riding or race conditions you expect to encounter, and ride.

In order to determine whether a race or ride you will be doing is going to have wet roots, I would suggest you either go to the Internet and do some research on the area or call one of the local bike shops. Bike shops can be a great resource for trails and trail conditions not to mention group rides. With that said, you can almost ensure that anything east of the Rockies will have wet roots, along with Oregon and Washington state. The farther you head east, the more dense the trees become. If you will be traveling to a NORBA National or World Cup race, chances are there is a description of the course on the promoter's Web site. If not, get out a map or atlas or go on the Internet and check out the terrain and the elevation, the density of trees, and find out the average rainfall for the time of year you will be there. Another good resource is your fellow racers. If you know someone who has been to the area before or done that race in the past, they can give you an idea of what you will be up against. Once you find out that a course will have wet roots, it is time to start practicing. If you plan on doing all of the races in the NORBA Nationals or any of the World Cup races, I suggest you start working on the skills I discuss next.

THE OBSTACLE COURSE

PURPOSE

To practice riding wet roots over dry terrain.

WARM-UP

Ride for 15-20 minutes at an easy pace.

TECHNIQUE

Line up branches or a garden hose perpendicular along the road, trail, or designated path in a lot near you. Start by riding over the branches or hose at a right angle.

1. First practice unweighting the front wheel when you first hit the obstacle and then unweight the rear wheel once the front wheel has cleared the obstacle (see figures 5.3a-b). (Unweighting simply means shift your weight back when the front wheel hits and shift your weight forward when the back wheel hits.) The movement should be small and not jerky. You don't want the wheels to come up; you just want to be light when you go over the roots.

2. Make sure you are not grabbing the brakes and look ahead about 3 feet.

a

Figure 5.3   *(a)* Unweighting the front tire.

(continued)

b

Figure 5.3 *(continued)* *(b)* Unweighting the rear tire.

3. Once you feel comfortable going over the obstacles with them at right angles to your wheels, mix them up so they are at all angles as well as close together. Continue to use the same techniques as above, unweighting, looking ahead, and not using your brakes.

4. Wet the obstacles and try riding over them performing the techniques as above.

TIPS

The best way to practice this skill is to exaggerate the motions.

GOING OUT ON THE TRAIL

PURPOSE

To practice riding wet roots on the trail.

WARM-UP

Ride your bike 15-20 minutes to a trail. If you are driving to the trailhead, try to get a 15-20 minute ride on a section that is not technical. I would even go so far as to ride on the road for 15 minutes before getting on the trail.

TECHNIQUE

Find a section of trail that has dry roots. Get off your bike and walk the sections and look at the various lines through the roots. Pick the line that has the least amount of roots, which in most cases is close to the tree.

1. As you come up to the roots, brake just before you hit them or feather your brakes, and unweight the front and then the rear wheel while looking ahead. Practice this several times before you move to the next step.

2. After you feel comfortable on dry roots, find a trail or section of trail that has wet roots. It is best to start small, with one or two wet roots that you can hit at right angles. Once you feel comfortable on one or two wet roots, add in a bigger section.

If there is not a trail in your area that has wet roots, it would behoove you to drive a short distance to find a trail with roots.

SAND PITS

Sandy conditions, similar to loose and dry conditions, can be very taxing if you aren't comfortable with this terrain. Tires and tire pressure are key in allowing you to get traction in sandy conditions. Having a smooth pedal stroke is also imperative if you plan to stay upright. Finally, speed is a crucial factor for both entering into a sandy section as well as riding through. If you have aspirations to ride the Poison Spider Trail in Moab, either go in the rainy season or hone your sand riding skills!

• Get the right tires for loose or sandy trails. Sandy conditions are very similar to the loose and dry conditions, but can be even more difficult. It is important to run tires with lugs that have a good amount of space in between them to allow some traction. Just think of a paddleboat going through the water: It needs a platform or paddle to propel the boat forward. With tires in the sand, you need rubber platforms to propel your bike forward.

Having less air in the tires also helps in the sandy sections. As in the loose conditions, less air in the tires gives more surface area in contact with the terrain, creating more paddles in the sand to propel the bike forward. If the tire compound is soft, it can also give more traction. Lastly, if you know the trail you will be riding is mostly loose sand, you may want to invest in a larger diameter tire. Just like an inflated inner tube on water, the larger tire will keep you riding higher on the surface of the sand, keeping you from bogging down. The only way you will make it through a long sandy section is by having a smooth pedal stroke. This means constant pressure on the pedals and even pressure throughout the stroke. If you have a choppy pedal stroke at all, your rear tire will kick out and you will be off and running.

• Control your speed in sandy sections. When you enter a sand pit, speed is crucial. If you hit the sand pit too quickly, you are likely to get catapulted off your bike because the sand will slow the bike while you keep moving forward. In fact, the faster you approach the sand pit, the more it will slow you down. It is as if your front tire is hitting a brick wall. On the other hand, if you are going too slowly when you hit the sand, you will bog down and simply roll to a stop. I can't give you an exact speed at which to enter a sandy wash, but you need to have enough momentum that your bike will keep moving forward once you impact. You should either be pedaling while you enter the sand or begin pedaling as soon as both of your tires are submerged to continue the forward momentum. In order to learn the appropriate speed at which to enter a sand pit, you need to practice your skills. You can do this by experimenting with different speeds or practice the drills I have laid out for you on page 84.

While in Moab, Utah, on the Amasa Back Trail, you run into several washes or gullies that contain a riverbed of sand. In this case you are headed downhill, so you need to lower your speed before you enter the gully and begin pedaling as soon as your front tire hits to keep your momentum. Coming back from the Gold Bar Rim Trail in Moab, you encounter several long stretches of sand that can span a quarter mile. On these sandy sections you need to brake less because you are entering from a flat surface. However, you still need to brake lightly so as not to hit the sand too hard on entry. Again, once your front tire hits the sand, it is time to start pedaling.

• Position your body for the impact. What position would you want to be in if you were to hit a brick wall with your bike? Yes, you would want to brace yourself. How would you do that? By getting as far back as possible so that when you hit you have time to stop your body's forward momentum before it hits the wall. That example may be a bit drastic, but it is the same idea. You need to get your hips and rear back behind the saddle with your center of gravity as low as possible. Visualize sitting down in a kitchen chair; that position is the one you want. You are driving your bike into the sand first, so just be ready for your bike to slow down quite rapidly.

Once both tires are in the sand, you should go back to putting equal pressure on the front and rear wheels. Do so by sitting on the saddle but keeping a good amount of weight on your upper body and therefore over the front tire. Keeping pressure on the front tire helps to keep the front tire tracking in a straight line. Keeping pressure on the rear tire ensures that it will stay in contact with the sand and continue to propel you forward. It is also important to keep a firm grip on the bars in sandy terrain. This does not mean that your upper body should be rigid; it means you want to be firm enough with the bars to control any jerky movement. Because of the increased density of the sand, the effect is that your front wheel is being pushed to the left and right.

Lastly, if all else fails: Run! When the sand is really deep, it will sap all of your strength to try to ride through it. The only true way of telling how deep a sand pit will be is to either ride or walk through it. In some instances you will see where other riders, cars, or walkers have gone through the sand and by looking at their tread, you can determine the depth of the sand. The track that shows less depth in the sand is the best course to take. However, running with your bike can be an energy saving option. Sometimes running will get you there faster than trying to ride.

The most obvious way to help your sand riding skills is to find a sand pit and ride through it. Start off with a small section and increase the size as you become more proficient. If you don't have sand close by deep, loose dirt and gravel are very similar. Riding on a gravel road is very much like riding in the sand. Better yet, like riding the gravel or dirt road on your road bike. Because the tires on your road bike are thinner, it will magnify the effect of the loose dirt or gravel, making it very similar to riding in deep sand on your mountain bike. Also, because riding through the sand takes a lot of strength and a smooth pedal stroke, performing the strength and endurance drills mentioned in the training section in chapter 2 will also help get your body get ready for any sand riding.

UPON ENTRY

PURPOSE
To build your maneuvering skills through sand with practice on a gravel road.

WARM-UP
Ride at least 15-20 minutes to the gravel road. Practice smoothing your pedal stroke on the way. You will need to have good circular motion to be more efficient in the gravel or sand.

TECHNIQUE
Find a road that has a short gravel sections and then work up to riding longer sections. When coming in to a gravel section you want to scrub your speed, meaning to slow down, before you enter. Scan the width of the road or trail and pick a line where the depth of the gravel is the least.

1. Enter the gravel by getting your rear off and slightly behind the saddle, which will keep you from being thrown forward when you hit.

2. Once you feel comfortable with the slower speed, practice entering the gravel at a higher speed with your body in the same position.

TIPS

Keep a firm but gentle grip on your bars. You don't want to force the front wheel to go where you want it to; it is better to coax it.

TOUCH DOWN AND PEDALING THROUGH

PURPOSE

To learn the appropriate pedaling technique for gravel rides.

WARM-UP

Warm up by riding 15-20 minutes before starting this exercise.

TECHNIQUE

Before you hit the gravel make sure you are in a moderately hard gear (e.g., middle chainring in the front and middle to lower cog in the back) so you don't have to shift once you are in. Also being in the appropriate gear will keep you from getting bogged down and coming off your bike. Once both tires are submerged in the gravel, sit down on the saddle and begin pedaling. Concentrate on making circles with your pedals while staying in a fairly hard gear. It's all about power. While keeping a good powerful pedal stroke, gently steer your bike or simply keep it on the line that you have chosen. Keeping a very light grip on the bars, guiding the bike should it start to veer off line. Avoid jerky movements on the bars or you will likely stop your front tire and get pitched off.

TIPS

Start this skill on a small patch of gravel and build to a longer one. Play with the different gears while pedaling through the gravel. It is natural to want to spin in an easy gear but you will be amazed how smoothly you can get through the gravel if you stay in a harder gear.

GO PLAY IN THE SANDBOX

PURPOSE

To hone your sand riding skills using a sand pit.

WARM-UP

Ride to the trailhead or do a 15-20 minute warm-up on a road or hard-packed trail.

TECHNIQUE

Start off with a small section of sand and increase the size as you become more proficient. Practice your entering skills (see drill Upon Entry and

Touch Down). Continue to work on longer and deeper sections of sand. When you are working on riding through sand, start with low tire pressure of around 35 lbs. After you are comfortable riding through a long stretch of sand, try pumping up your tires to 45+ lbs. This will help to make you a sand pit expert!

TIPS

Always end on a positive note. If you are having trouble mastering the technique or are becoming frustrated, run through the sandy section and end the ride on a road or trail that you feel comfortable with.

ROCKS

Some of the most common rocky conditions you will encounter on your mountain bike are slick rock and baby head rocks. Slick rock is a large, flat expanse of rock with a fairly smooth surface and is most often connected with riding in Moab, Utah. Baby head rocks are generally rocks from the size of grapefruits to watermelons. They can either be secure in the ground or be loose. Generally you find these types of rocks in a rock garden or big grouping. The classic baby head rock sighting was in the NORBA National event in Pennsylvania. There were several casualties on that course specifically affecting kneecaps.

Slick Rock

Slick rock is an amazing surface to ride on because your tires seem to grip the surface. It is possible to ride up a 45-degree slope or on the edge of a rocky ledge without falling off. However, this terrain is not for the beginner rider. On my first excursion to Moab, I was riding with a group of friends who were of all levels and abilities. We decided to ride the slick rock trail because it is the most noted trail in Moab. We got halfway around the loop when one of the riders crashed and sustained a gaping gash in her shin. Luckily I was riding with a group of physical therapy and medical students who were smart enough to carry a first-aid kit. We bandaged her up pretty well and then got her to the medical clinic in town when we finished the ride. She came back with a good amount of stitches. The stories about breaking bones and being airlifted out of Moab are plentiful. The key to riding slick rock is trusting your tires to grip the surface and learning to shift your weight or stand and pedal when necessary.

A huge part of the attraction of riding slick rock is the rider's ability to climb up what appears to be the face of cliffs without falling off. This phenomenon occurs because of your tires' ability to stick to the surface of the rock without slipping. Okay, the description of slick rock is a little deceiving. Although it sounds as if slick rock would be slippery, it is actually a larger, flat rock that has the surface of sandpaper but looks smooth. Sometimes, as with the Rim Trail in Moab, the whole trail is basically made up of one humongous rock. Unlike most other conditions, slick rock is unmoving and has little to no loose material on its surface. This allows for continuous traction of your tire to the surface of the rock. When coming up on a trail that gives you a choice of riding on either slick rock or loose dirt, always choose to ride the rock. Because you know you will get good traction, you can also get more speed on slick rock as well as not worry about skidding out or going down.

Because slick rock allows for a lot of traction, your ability to pedal while standing is enormous. When you stand and pedal, you can get more power and weight behind the pedal stroke. With both the awesome traction and increased power, a rider is able to crank up steep hills. Smooth pedal stroke is not as much of a factor on slick rock either because it has no loose dirt to throw you off.

Many weight shifting skills exist for riding on slick rock. As with going up any steep climb, you need to shift more weight on to the rear wheel to keep traction on the drive wheel. With the ability to go up steeper climbs, you also must watch for the front tire lifting off the ground. To counteract this effect, you need to keep enough weight forward. In effect, you should look as if you are lying on the top tube. Because your head weighs as much as a bowling ball, if you bring your head forward and over your bars, you should have enough weight to keep the front wheel down. By getting your hips back on the saddle, you should have enough weight on the rear wheel (see figure 5.4). Again, this skill takes practice.

Figure 5.4 To climb slick rock, distribute your weight evenly so there is adequate pressure on the front and the rear tires.

RIDING ROCK GARDENS

Travis Brown

© Courtesy of Trek Bicycles

"Riding rock gardens can be a great way to gain seconds on your competition. It can also hand them the advantage if you bobble and have to run anyway. The key in these situations is even momentum. There will be many crux rocks that you will clean at 5 mph that will stop you cold at 3 mph. I usually like to ride a gear that is a bit bigger than what I am comfortable turning over to reduce potential wheelspin. This is a technique that I learned through cleaning section on my single speed that I never had on a geared bike. It is important to know if a rock garden has the potential to give an advantage over the competition; if so, lead into that section. It is better to go for a section that you are not assured of making from a leading position so that you won't get gapped if you come off the bike. Conversely, I am never too proud to run a section of rock if I know that I will gain two seconds over my competitor who bobbles in the middle of a section. Each rider needs to make their own risk/benefit analysis on a given section and approach it in a way that fits their strengths or exploits the competitions weaknesses."

RIDING THE ROCK FACE WHILE SEATED

PURPOSE

To practice riding up slick rock while in a sitting position.

WARM-UP

Take a 15-20 minute ride on pavement riding on flat to rolling hills.

TECHNIQUE

Find a steep paved road or cement culvert or ditch that is safe to ride on. Put some slick or semislick tires on your mountain bike (tires that have little to no tread and pump them up to 35 lbs). The lower the pressure, the more surface area of the tire on the terrain, meaning more stick.

Get some speed up while coming up to the steep climb and then practice climbing in a seated position. Scoot your rear forward in the saddle and bend your arms keeping your shoulders close to the bars. Stay in a moderately easy gear, middle chainring, and one of the five biggest cogs in the back. Slick rock gives you the opportunity to shift while riding it but it is best to start off in a bit bigger gear and shift higher or to an easier gear.

TIPS

Remain seated as long as you can while riding the face of the climb. If you find yourself slowing down too much, stand up briefly at the top of the climb just to get you over the lip.

RIDING THE ROCK FACE WHILE STANDING UP

PURPOSE

To practice riding slick rock in a standing position.

WARM-UP

Warm up by riding for 15–20 minutes.

TECHNIQUE

Get some speed up before you get to the climb. Start in a moderate gear position your rear on the saddle. Once you feel your speed starts to slow, say 200–300 feet up the hill, stand up and pedal. Where you stand will depend on the pitch of the climb but you don't want to wait until you have lost too much speed or you won't be able to make it up the climb. Make a smooth transition from sitting to standing and keep the momentum going.

TIPS

Stand with your hips just over or bit behind the saddle, bend your elbows, and keep your shoulders close to the bars. This is a similar position as climbing steep loose terrain but you will find you don't have to worry as much about the rear tire sliding out, it *sticks*! Practice this several times on different inclines and in different gearing until you feel comfortable.

TAKE IT TO THE ROCK

PURPOSE

To practice rock riding on actual rock.

TECHNIQUE

Find a trail near you or make a trip to Moab, Utah, and practice your slick rock skills. Begin on flat surfaces and short, gradual climbs working on your seated position. Practice that same climb going from seated to standing position (figure 5.5). Once you feel comfortable on short climbs, begin to increase the length of the climb and the steepness of the pitch.

TIPS

Start with your tires less inflated (35-40 lbs) and increase the pressure once you feel comfortable. Riding slick rock is truly about being confident that your tires will stick in more drastic inclines and declines.

Figure 5.5 Climbing in the standing position.

Baby Head Rocks

Riding baby head rocks is all about strength and speed. If you are riding a full-suspension bike, you have a greater possibility of being able to sit while riding, which is a huge advantage for energy conservation. If you are still old school, like myself, and you don't own a full-suspension cross-country ride, you will be spending more time out of the saddle and pedaling. Independent of which type of bike you ride, you will need to get to the gym to conquer baby heads. Riding on secure baby heads is like doing 20 to 30 repetitions of single-leg squats. To avoid getting bounced around, you need to stand just over the saddle while pedaling. Can you say leg burn?! And don't forget the need for speed. The more speed you have, the less likely you are to feel the bumps, so you need to try to keep a moderate pace throughout the ride. As with most technical skills, there is a fine line between going too fast and too slow. Don't go bombing into the first rocky section to launch yourself over the bars. A rock can stop you dead in your tracks if you hit it going full bore. Try to keep a moderate pace when coming up on a rock garden and keep that same pace throughout, and you will come out of it unscathed. Lastly, I wasn't kidding when I said you should get to the gym. You need to do squats, lunges, and step-ups. These exercises will help you to get stronger, and strength is definitely a factor in many aspects of mountain biking.

As previously discussed, the way to initiate a riding skill is to start small. Find a rock garden that is 5 feet long and work your way up to a 20-foot rock garden. Practice entering at a moderate pace, meaning around 10 miles an hour, and keeping that speed while you pedal through the rocks. Stay slightly off the saddle and keep a smooth pedal stroke.

Another way to practice, especially for those of us who don't have many baby heads in the area, is to work on pedaling while standing. Make this into an interval. Get a good 20- to 30-minute warm-up and then stand up and ride, keeping a smooth pedal stroke for 2 to 5 minutes. Sit down and pedal for 5 minutes and then stand again. Work your way up from 4 of these intervals to 7 or 8.

When I say stand while pedaling, I don't mean completely up and over the pedal spindle while transferring your weight, which is the typical method while standing. This style of riding demands that you do more of a crouch over your saddle to keep your center of gravity low and keep the bike from bobbing side to side. You should keep your hips directly over or slightly forward on the saddle and then lift your body about 1 or 2 inches off the saddle while pedaling

STANDING FOR BABY HEADS

PURPOSE

To practice riding baby head rocks while standing.

WARM-UP

Get into a good 15-30 minute easy spin before trying this skill.

TECHNIQUE

Find a dirt road or trail that has a flat surface and practice standing over your saddle while pedaling. Place your hips directly over or slightly in front of your seated position on the saddle (see figure 5.6). You should look like you are preparing to sit down in the saddle but keeping your body 1-2 inches above the saddle. Practice pedaling without bobbing or moving your body.

TIPS

Make this skill into an interval. Warm up for 15-30 minutes and then stand up and ride, keeping a smooth pedal stroke, for 2-5 minutes. Sit down and pedal for 5 minutes and then stand again. Work your way up from 4 of these intervals to 7 or 8. In this interval you stay in a moderate to hard gear so that you have constant resistance on the pedals.

Figure 5.6 Crouch over the bike to maintain momentum and equal weight distribution over the tires.

GETTING A HEAD

PURPOSE
To practice riding baby heads on real rock.

WARM-UP
Ride for 15-30 minutes practicing your body position and pedal technique along the way.

TECHNIQUE
Start small. Find a rock garden that is 5 feet long and work your way up to a 20-foot long rock garden. Enter the rock section at a slow speed keeping that pace throughout while standing and pedaling. Once you feel comfortable at a slow speed, enter at a faster speed and keep that pace up. It is much easier it is to ride on rocks at a higher speed. It is a smoother ride and you don't have to worry as much about picking a line. Never enter at high speeds or you will get catapulted off and that is when your kneecap gets fractured.

TIPS
If you don't have anything remotely similar to a rock garden, the next best thing is to find a grassy field that is full of bumps and divots. This closely simulates the rock garden and forces you to pedal while in the same position, especially if you are on a cyclo-cross bike!

WATER

Depending on where you live, you may encounter a bit of water in rivers and streams. My home of Colorado is a mostly dry state, so water isn't something that we mountain bikers deal with on a daily or even weekly basis. But if I lived on the East Coast or in the Northwest, water would be an everyday occurrence.

As a beginning mountain biker, my standard technique for river crossing was to close my eyes and hold my breath, something you should never do. I can remember my brother laughing at me while watching me cross a river on the trail out of Fairfax, California, as I rode through the water looking like a blowfish. The proper way to cross water is to enter at the correct speed; use a smooth, continuous pedal stroke while in the water; and pick a line with the least number of rocks.

Speed of Entry

Speed of entry is a key part of riding through a river crossing. Many riders, especially beginners, think the best method is to go plunging in at high speeds. What better way to keep your momentum and get out as fast as possible? I can tell you from experience that this method does not work, especially if you have no idea what is in the river. I will never forget the river crossing in the National race and Helena, Georgia, in 1996 and 1997. This course was notoriously wet and muddy and the whole area gave off the aroma of horse manure. I found out later that the smell came from microorganisms in the soil; you know, those little beings that can cause infections. After slogging around the muddy course we came careening into a river crossing. I generally looked forward to this part of the course because the water was warm and it would help rid my bike and my body of excess mud. The first time I came barreling into the water, I plowed right into a rock and went rear over teakettle, with my rear tire coming up over my head, and I ended up face first in the water. I promptly jumped up and continued on my path around the course with several bleeding appendages. My next foray into the water crossing, I had a kinder, gentler approach and pedaled through with no problem. The water crossing did come back to haunt me in the form of a plum on my kneecap. After several months of trying everything to get rid of the lump on my knee that turned up after my crash wounds had healed, I finally went to an orthopedist who told me I had an infection and needed antibiotics. Because of all the bacteria in the soil and water at the Georgia racecourse, I got an infection when I crashed. So learn from my mistakes—don't go careening in to a river crossing; and if you do, try to keep your skin intact at all cost!

Entry and Follow-Through

The right technique for riding a water crossing is to lightly brake before entering the water. Anything lying in the water, such as a rock or big root, can stop you dead if you are going too fast. And because water is a more dense substance than air, entering a water crossing can feel like hitting a wall if you are going too fast. To lessen the impact of the water, enter it at a slower speed. Another reason to slow down upon entry is that it will allow you to see possible obstacles in the water. It is almost impossible to see anything in the water unless you are directly on top of it. When you are in the open air you can look 5 to 10 feet ahead of you and down the trail, but in the water you can only see 1 or 2 feet ahead of you so you need to slow your speed to pick the best line through the water.

Once you have entered the water, you need to keep your momentum by getting a good, smooth pedal stroke going. Riding through water is similar to riding through sand, which means you need to pedal to make it through without coming to a complete stop. Water will give you more resistance when you are pedaling, but you can still make headway and pick out obstacles by going more slowly and maneuvering through. It is

CROSSING STREAMS

Adam Craig

© Tom Moran/STPHOTO.com

"In my mind there are two types of stream crossings—the one you bomb through with your eyes half closed, such as Tipperary Creek, and the type you ride into slow and pick a line around the rocks and try to make it through.

For the Blind Bomber crossing, ride into the stream as fast as you can muster and—now this is the only part that requires anything except commitment—pick a point ten feet past the other side of the body of water and focus on it; don't even look into the water, since you won't see that rock with will take you out anyway! Just hope for the best and ride it out. This technique is not recommended for days below 55 degrees! On those days exercise the sheepish rock hop/bike outrigger technique, hopping from rock to rock with your bike as a crutch.

For the skillful crossing, roll up to the water slowly but committed, quickly scope out the smoothest line around whatever obstacles you see (and maybe a dry place to dab if need be), and roll on in. Once in the water, it's very important to maintain momentum. It's also key to have a very light touch with every input you make, pedal a gear or two taller and very softly, brake gently if at all, and only make minor direction changes. You're dealing with very slippery rocks and pretty much any input to the bike other than momentum maintenance will result in slipping and a wet foot. Finesse and feel is the key, be soft, but not soggy."

---

another condition where having some power and strength in your legs will help propel you forward.

Most river crossings will start on a downhill because water generally runs through a low-lying gorge. To keep your speed down, you should be feathering the brakes. You should not be fully stopped, but your front wheel should slice through the water when you enter. And if you slow your speed when coming to a denser substance, you will lessen the impact. I know this advice is counterintuitive and the instinct is to blast into the water, but don't do it. Once your front tire is submerged, start pedaling to ensure that you don't come to a complete stop. You will be amazed at your ability to pedal through a moderately flowing river, where the water comes up to your skewers and isn't running too fast. If you are not sure what the skewer is, refer to the bike diagram in chapter 1. If you are questioning your ability to ride it, get off your bike and run.

Once you have successfully entered the water, the pedaling process begins. I can't stress enough that you also need a smooth pedal stroke to propel your bike through the water. It is more of a power stroke, so you want to be in a middle gear. Once your bike is in the water, you will be able to ride over obstacles that would not be doable on dry land because of the increased buoyancy. Using a choppy stroke, you will be kicking up scud and debris from the bottom of the river and most likely lose traction. With a smooth stroke, you will be able to propel your bike through the water as well as over any obstacles you encounter in the river.

Picking a Line

When you are entering a river or body of water, you should be scanning for rocks and obstacles. Usually you can see the contents of the water directly in front of you unless other riders have gone ahead of you and muddied the view. Not creating waves or going too fast upon entry will ensure a clear view of the contents after you have entered so you can pick a path with fewer rocks. Be aware that you will not be able to do much steering once in the water because of the increase in density. You can make small adjustments, but don't make jerky movement on the bars, or you will stop your forward momentum and crash. The best method is to choose a line and stick with it. Keep the bars steady and look 1 or 2 feet ahead. Don't panic if you see a large rock in your path; stay the course. The rocks and obstacles are magnified when looking through the water. As I mentioned before, you will also be able to ride over larger obstacles with less difficulty because of your increased buoyancy while in the water. If the water is murky, pick a straight path to the other side and pedal. Believe you can make it, and you will.

Again, always start small. If possible, find a creek near your home that you can take time to practice on. Get off your bike at the edge of the creek before entering, and look for a line. Once you pick your line, go back at least 20 feet and remount. This is to give you plenty of time to get your feet in the clips and pick up some speed before entering the water. Once you have mastered the creek crossing, find a creek or river that is a bit larger to challenge yourself. You don't have to worry as much about crashing or falling over in a river; the force of impact when crashing in water is much less than if you were to crash on dirt. However, the chill factor can be a problem.

You can also benefit from following a more seasoned rider through a river crossing. Watch their speed and what line they choose, and mimic what they do. If they can do it, you can too.

STARTING SMALL

PURPOSE
To practice crossing small, shallow waterways.

WARM-UP
Warm up for 15-30 minutes.

TECHNIQUE
Begin on a creek or section of river that is not to deep or wide. Get off your bike at the edge of the creek before entering and look for a line. Once you pick your line, go back at least 20 feet and remount your bike. Before entering the creek, feather your brakes slightly to slow you down. Position your body so your hips are above and behind the saddle and you are effectively pushing your bike in to the water in front of you. After both tires are in the water, sit back down on your saddle and begin pedaling. Stay in a moderately hard gear, middle chainring and one of the four biggest cogs

in the back to help keep your speed up while riding through the water. See figure 5.7.

TIPS

Pedaling through the water really is a combination of riding through the sand and riding on baby heads because the resistance is similar. Practice your sand and rocks skills before trying water crossings.

Figure 5.7 Once in the water, keep up your speed and let the bike slice through the water.

GOING BIG

PURPOSE

To practice crossing wide waterways.

WARM-UP

Warm up for 15-30 minutes.

TECHNIQUE

Go to the edge of the river and look for the line. Once you have determined where you are going to enter, back up about 20 feet and ready yourself to enter the river by feathering your brakes and getting in the correct position. After both tires are in the water, sit down in the saddle or hover just over the saddle and begin pedaling. Once the river gets 2 to 3 feet deep, you will probably have to run it. Remember, the good thing about practicing your river crossings is you don't have to worry as much about crashing or falling over. The impact when crashing in water is much less than if you were to crash on dirt; however, the chill factor can be a problem.

TIPS

Follow a more seasoned rider through a river crossing. Watch their speed and what line they choose and mimic what they do. Or watch videos of mountain bike races. Check the positions of the riders and how they pedal before you attempt to ride one.

Mountain biking, being the great sport that it is, is made up of a multitude of terrain and the skills that go along with it. Becoming an excellent mountain bike racer and rider requires that you become a master on all terrain. After having finished this chapter and diligently practiced the skills, you will be well on your way to standing on the podium.

SIX

Breaking Loose on the Flats

In general, mountain bikers tend to slow down when they come to a flat section, so your friends and fellow racers will be impressed when you learn to power through them. You will need to learn to fight the tendency to slow down, but what you need most for speed on the flat sections is power. This chapter will give you some ideas on the technical aspects of riding flats, motor pacing, and then measuring your progress.

THE TECHNICAL STUFF

For me, the flat sections were always the place where I would regroup and catch my breath. This attitude was fine when I was a sport and expert racer, but once I joined the pro class, I found myself getting passed by other racers on the flat sections. Because my goal was to be the fastest rider on the course, I had to overcome my inertia in the flat sections and learn to keep my speed throughout the whole race. Changing how you think while riding does not happen overnight; as many experienced riders will tell you, it is a constant work in progress.

- Keep the speed. Riding fast on the flat sections really comes in to play when you, as a racer, are trying to shave 30 seconds to 3 minutes off your time. When you start to move up the ranks in your category, be it sport, expert or pro, it will become important to utilize every opportunity to make time on your fellow racers. If you are a good climber and descender, you have won two thirds of the battle. The problem arises when you are racing against others that not only can climb and descend but are also motoring on the flat sections.

First, you have to give up the idea of taking a break on the flat sections. Of course, at times you need to catch your breath, but those times end up being 30-second intervals throughout the course or while on a less technical downhill section. As mountain bikers, we need to change the way we view flat sections. Instead of seeing them as a break and slowing down, use the flat sections as a place to get some time on the racer behind you or close the gap on the racer in front of you. The only way to change a habit is by weeks and months and even years of practice. Just like anything that is important, you have to work at it. Power on!

- Stay smooth. To keep my speed up on the flat sections, I concentrate on keeping a smooth pedal stroke. It gives me something to focus on instead of just being tired. You can also focus on the person ahead of you and visualize getting closer and or passing them. Or, if you work better when being chased, visualize that the person behind you is gaining on you to motivate you to keep up your pace.

Smoothing out your pedal stroke has a whole different meaning when on flat terrain. You don't do it to help keep traction, but rather to ensure you have power throughout the stroke. You should also shift to a bigger gear to increase your speed. Basically you need to find the cadence that feels most comfortable to you. Get in to the biggest gear possible that allows you to keep a comfortable cadence while keeping your pedal stroke smooth (see figure 6.1). If your stroke gets choppy, you become less efficient and you lose energy. Visualize a steam engine with the pistons running smoothly. Another good visual is to think about closing the gap on the rider in front of you.

Figure 6.1 Keep your speed up on the flats.

• Power through. To get faster on the flats, it is essential that you do drills on the flats. You can do these drills on a mountain or road bike, but it is often less taxing on the rider to train on the road as you don't have the jarring effect of the rough terrain or as much upper body involvement. In fact, as I will mention in future chapters, mountain bike racers do around 70 percent of their training on the road, on a road bike.

GOING FAST ON THE FLATS

Alison Dunlap

© Sport the Library

"Going fast on the flats is a mix of speed and power. You need to push bigger gears to generate higher watts (i.e., power), but you can't be in such a big gear that you fatigue prematurely. A lot of your power comes from your glutes when you time trial on the flats. Don't be afraid to really utilize all muscles in your legs and lower back. Your cadence will vary depending on the terrain. Flat trails with a tail wind will be much faster and you may even be spun out. If you feel yourself slowing down or getting bogged down, stand up and sprint for a few seconds. This will increase your speed and give you a bit of an adrenalin boost to keep your legs going."

The two basic intervals I work on with my athletes, and the intervals I performed when I was racing, are lactate threshold and $\dot{V}O_2$. The physiology of these intervals will be discussed in detail in chapter 10. This section is designed simply to give you the basic idea behind intervals to do on the flat sections. In general, lactate threshold are moderately paced intervals that should be similar to the average pace you go during a race. $\dot{V}O_2$ intervals, on the other hand are to get you to go as hard as you can for 2 to 8 minutes at a time. This is not to be confused with a sprint, which is an 8- to 30-second, all-out effort.

TESTING LACTATE THRESHOLD

PURPOSE

To increase your ability to tolerate and clear lactic acid and to conquer your inertia on the flats.

WARM-UP

Warm up for 15-20 minutes before starting this exercise.

TECHNIQUE

Find a flat section of road or fire road where you can go for at least 5 minutes. Get into a big gear and ride for 5-30 minutes at a moderate pace, followed by 5-20 minutes at an easy pace. Make sure that you are keeping a smooth pedal stroke, concentrating on getting a circular motion with your feet and pedals. Don't overdo it or make it stressful. You should feel comfortable with this pedal stroke and at this pace.

$\dot{V}O_2$ DRILL

PURPOSE

To increase your ability to work at submax effort for short intervals.

WARM-UP

Warm up for 15-20 minutes at an easy pace.

TECHNIQUE

After warming up, go as hard as you can for 3 to 7 minutes before taking a 3- to 7-minute easy spin in between each. Concentrate on keeping a smooth pedal stroke and not mashing or pushing down too hard on the downstroke. This interval is obviously more difficult, but do it with efficiency in mind. These exercises will help with your ability to push harder on flat sections by performing them on flat sections on the road or mountain.

MOTOR PACING

Motor pacing is an excellent way to increase your speed on flat surfaces. It was rumored that Paola Pezzo did most of her training for the 1996 Olympics by motor pacing with her coach. I can attest to the fact that she did quite a bit of motor pacing. I recall watching her motor pace before some of the World Cup races in 2000 to warm up for the races.

Motor pacing is a form of training in which the cyclist follows close behind a motor scooter or car, effectively getting a draft from the vehicle. It is done on flat to rolling surfaces and obviously only done on the road. Drafting allows the cyclist to go at faster speeds while pushing a big gear because the vehicle or rider ahead is displacing the wind or punching a hole through the air ahead of the rider. The benefits of motor pacing are as follows: The cyclist becomes more comfortable sitting on the wheel of a fast moving vehicle, they become more comfortable going at higher speeds, they become more efficient at pushing a big gear, and it forces them to increase their power.

Practice gaining speed on flat surfaces by following a faster cyclist or a scooter or car.

Compared to road cycling, mountain biking does not have many situations that require a cyclist to draft another cyclist. However, it does happen. Drafting means sitting just inches away from the wheel of the rider ahead of you. According to Edmund Burke, while drafting, a cyclist can consume 30-40 percent less energy than those leading the pace line or pack. When a cyclist was drafting at 20 mph (on the road), $\dot{V}O_2$ was reduced by 18 percent compared to riding alone. At 25 mph, the benefit was considerably greater, saving 26 percent. Motor pacing is similar to drafting a fellow cyclist but at higher speeds and getting a much better draft or wind break. Becoming comfortable with motor pacing will help you learn how close you can sit behind a cyclist and what is the best position to be in depending on where the wind is coming from.

When motor pacing, the vehicle can reach speeds far higher than those of a single cyclist. A peloton, or group of racing cyclists, can go at speeds of 50 miles per hour. But unless you have a group of friends at your disposal to pull you around, motor pacing is a good alternative. By following a scooter going at 35 to 45 miles per hour, you will definitely become more comfortable going at a high rate of speed.

Motor pacing forces you to push the biggest gear possible. There is no way to stay in the draft if you are in a small gear. You also need to keep up your speed to stay on a wheel. If you have ever sat behind a fast-moving cyclist, you have most likely experienced the effect of falling out of the draft. Once you get 10 to 12 inches behind the wheel of the cyclist ahead of you, you will no longer benefit from them punching a hole in the wind, and the effect is rapid loss of contact with the rider. Once you have lost contact, it is almost impossible to get back on their wheel. The consequences of getting dropped should motivate you to endure a bit more pain and increase your power output.

MOTOR PACE WITH CONFIDENCE

PURPOSE

To become more confident in your ability to motor pace.

WARM-UP

Ride for 15-30 minutes at an easy pace before hooking up with the pace vehicle in order to get your body ready for higher speeds.

TECHNIQUE

Before you try motor pacing behind a vehicle, get comfortable riding behind the wheel of another rider. Find a rider that is faster than you are or can push the pace for 10-20 minutes and sit 1-2 inches behind their wheel. Once you can do this comfortably without falling off the rider's wheel, you will be ready to try it behind a motorized vehicle. Keep in mind that this may take months to be comfortable with, and don't rush it. Once you have mastered riding behind a strong road cyclist, you can move on to riding behind a motorized scooter. Start off by going at a slower speed, 20-25 miles per hour, and then have the driver speed up as you get more confidence.

TIPS

Make sure that the driver of the vehicle is skilled at motor pacing and can watch for hand signals. A thumbs up means the driver can speed up a bit and a thumbs down means slow down. Motor pacing is best done on a flat open road with little to no traffic. If you or your pace driver are not completely comfortable with the conditions, wait for another day!

MEASURING YOUR PROGRESS

You can measure your ability to increase speed on the flats using simple methods or with high-tech gadgets. The simple way to determine whether you are going faster on flat sections is to time yourself: Find a flat section of road or trail and time how long it takes to get from one point to another. The section of road or trail should take you at least 20 minutes to complete. Be sure to time yourself before you begin your training. Then once you have trained or practiced increasing your speed on the flats, time yourself on that same section of road or trail again. Take into account these factors every time you test yourself: time of day, weather conditions (wind, temperature), your weight, the last time you ate or drank, and what and how much you consumed. You may also want to measure your rate of perceived exertion during the test. When timing yourself if these factors are significantly different, they may alter the outcome.

A more specific way of testing your progress is to use a speedometer, heart rate monitor, or watt meter (see chapter 9 for more information on these devices). With a speedometer, you should designate a specific stretch of road or trail that you will test yourself on. Clock your average speed early in the training season and then again after you have trained for several weeks. If you have progressed, your average speed should have gone up. The averages will be different for each individual. The novice athlete should make bigger gains while the highly trained athlete may only see smaller increases in their average speed with all other factors being fairly equal. If you are using a heart rate monitor as a training tool, you should notice that your average heart rate will be lower over the course of the timed test. Lastly, but definitely not least expensive, if you have access to a device that will measure your power output or watts, you should find you can push higher watts over the timed test.

It is important for mountain bike racers to be able to push the pace on their own. Many times in a race situation you won't have another rider in sight, which means you have to be self motivated to keep up the pace. The following drills will help you to get more comfortable pushing yourself on the flat sections of a mountain bike race.

GOING IT ALONE

PURPOSE
To gain confidence on riding through flat sections.

WARM-UP
Warm up for 15-30 minutes at a slow or easy pace. The longer the warm-up the better in order to get your body ready to perform at a higher pace.

TECHNIQUE
Find a long stretch of road that is flat to a little rolling. After warming up, shift to a moderate to hard gear and slowly increase your speed until you are at a level where you can no longer talk. You should be concentrating on keeping a smooth pedal stroke. This skill is similar to lactate threshold intervals. Start off by going for 5 minutes while in a moderately hard gear and keeping a smooth pedal stroke, then build up to 15-20 minute intervals.

Week 1: 2 days of 4 x 5 minute intervals with a 5-minute easy spin in between each.

Week 2: 2 days of 4 x 10 minute intervals with a 10-minute easy spin in between each.

Week 3: 2 days of 3 x 15 minute intervals with a 10-minute easy spin in between each.

Week 4: 2 days of 3 x 20 minute intervals with a 10- to 15-minute easy spin in between each.

TIPS
This skill should not be performed until you have been riding for 6-8 weeks. As you will learn in chapter 10, it is important to get some easy rides in before you start doing harder intervals. This is to ensure that you don't injure yourself when your body isn't prepared.

Sitting on the wheel of someone or a group of people who are a bit faster than you is a good way to push you to go faster on the flat sections. The easiest method of human motor pacing is to ride with fast friends or find a local road riding group (see figure 6.2). In Boulder, Colorado, it is not too hard to find a group ride leaving from various locations on a Saturday or Sunday morning. You can usually also find a ride leaving some time during the week. We put riding above working in this neck of the woods.

© Roving Photo

Figure 6.2 Push yourself on flat sections by working in a group.

The way to find these rides is to simply go out for a ride and start talking to all of the riders you meet. Another way to find a group ride in your area is to go to a local bike shop and ask.

GROUP RIDES

PURPOSE
To practice riding in groups.

WARM-UP
Ride for 15-20 minutes at an easy pace.

TECHNIQUE
Once you find a good group ride, or single rider that is willing to pull you around, go out with them 1 day a week. It is best to go out on a flat section of road, as this is what you are working on, but sitting on a wheel on rolling hills and climbs can't hurt. The object is to stay on the person's wheel

that is in front of you for as long as you can. Concentrate on smoothing out your pedal stroke, relaxing your upper body, and keeping an eye on their pedals or their rear wheel. It may take you several rides to be comfortable riding someone's wheel, but the more you do it the more comfortable you will feel. The stronger and more confident you get, the longer you will be able to stay with the rider or group.

TIPS

Experiment with your position behind the rider's wheel. Depending on the direction of the wind, sit 1-2 inches behind the rider's wheel. It is important to stay within that distance behind the rider and not yo-yo or create a gap and then close it. Be aware that there may be other people riding behind you and the more unsteady you are, the bigger the changes will be behind you, similar to the ripple effect.

Another method of working on being strong on flat sections of a mountain bike course is to enter a road time trial. Road time trials are generally on a flat to rolling section of road that last from 20 minutes to an hour. Because they are timed starts, where there is a 10 to 30 second space in between each rider, it forces you to stay focused on keeping your speed up and smoothing out your pedal stroke as there is no other rider's wheel to focus on.

THE DREADED TIME TRIAL

PURPOSE

To practice time trials by working on your speed and pedal stroke.

WARM-UP

Warm up for at least 30 minutes with some hard efforts before starting a time trial in order to get your lungs and legs ready to push a hard pace.

TECHNIQUE

Start the time trial by gradually building to a faster speed. If you sprint at the start you will find yourself out of breath before you get a minute into the race. This will force you to slow down again and lose time. Once you are up to cruising speed or at a pace you feel is just below cracking, concentrate on keeping a smooth pedal stroke and relaxing your upper body while pushing the hardest gear you can.

TIPS

Visualize yourself catching the person ahead of you. Try to keep your heart rate steady by checking yourself with a heart rate monitor.

Now that you have done your workouts on the road, take your skills to the dirt. The only way to truly get better at going fast on a flat section of road or trail is to ride on the same terrain. A fun way of getting stronger on the flats while riding your mountain bike is to make it in to a game.

TAKING IT TO THE DIRT

PURPOSE
To practice flats while riding the terrain.

WARM-UP
Warm up for 15-30 minutes at an easy spin.

TECHNIQUE
While riding with your friends or by yourself make a plan that any time you get to a flat section of trail you are going to go as fast as you can. If the trail is mostly flat, designate certain sections of the trail to pick up the pace.

TIPS
Make it fun! The more you enjoy what you are doing, the longer you are apt to do it.

To excel at mountain biking, you need to conquer all the skills it takes to go fast. One of these skills is going fast on the flat sections. If you have come from a road riding or racing background, you are probably already efficient at keeping the pace up on flat sections of the road or trail. If you are like me and started off riding mountain bikes and didn't purchase a road bike until after three years of racing mountain bikes, you may have to make an effort to practice riding fast on the flat sections.

SEVEN

Hoofing It Through Dangerous Spots

Sometimes you have to get off of your bike and make a run for it. It would be faster and safer to run in certain conditions such as sketchy downhills, steep and loose climbs, and when you're feeling insecure about riding over obstacles. Learning to mount, dismount, and run with your bike are skills needed for cyclo-cross racing, but they are also very important to mountain bike riding and racing. This chapter will teach you the proper techniques for dismounting, running with your bike, and remounting, along with some advice for practicing on obstacle courses, and information to help you decide whether the situation warrants that you run or ride.

I can recall the first time I decided I should learn how to get on and off my bike as fast as possible. It was that darn Vermont National again. The course took you over a technical rocky section and then over a short bridge. I and a few other racers spent at least 30 minutes trying to decide what we could and could not ride and where to dismount and mount. That afternoon I went back to the condo and had a fellow racer, Jergen Bergeron, teach me the correct method for getting on and off my bike. I was actually so excited about trying out my new skill that I was looking forward to the race.

THE DISMOUNT, RUN, AND REMOUNT

This technique is the same technique used in a cyclo-cross races. If you have ever entered or watched a cyclo-cross race (a bike race where you have to get off your bike and run as well as jump over barriers), you have an idea of the appropriate technique. Once I have talked you through the appropriate technique, I will give you some skills to go out and practice. It is always wise to find someone who is well versed in mounting and dismounting to watch you and give you some pointers

To dismount, swing one leg over the saddle while your bike is still in motion (see figure 7.1). You should generally go to the side that you are most comfortable with or have an easier time getting out of the pedals. I am left-handed and feel more comfortable standing and dismounting on my left side, and therefore I go through the sequence by swinging my right leg over the saddle. Once I swing my right leg around, I feed it between my left leg and the bike. At the same time I am swinging my right leg through, I take my right hand off of the bar and grab the middle of the top tube. When I am close enough to the running section, which should only be a lapse of 10 to15 seconds, I continue to step through with my right foot and at the same time flick my left foot out of the pedal. Once my right foot hits the ground I can either pick up my bike with my right hand and lift it over the obstacle, push the bike forward over the rough

Figure 7.1 Swing your nondominant leg over the bike while still in motion and feed it through your dominant leg and the bike once you are close to the running section.

terrain, or lift the bike up on to my shoulder and run with it in that position. It is best to wait until you are as close as possible to the obstacle or running section before you dismount because riding is faster than running and the more forward momentum you can keep by staying on your bike, the better.

In a long running section, you may decide to shoulder your bike, which will allow you to run faster. The appropriate technique for shouldering the bike is to put your right hand on the down tube instead of the top tube and use that hand to swing the bike up, planting the middle of the top tube on your shoulder (see figure 7.2). Then let go of the down tube and feed that arm through the frame triangle and back around between the frame and the fork and place it on the left side of the bars. Your left hand will then be free to swing in a running motion to help propel you forward. This may be difficult for those of us who have small frames because the water bottle cage will get in the way of you feeding your arm through the triangle. The other option for mountain bikers is to rest the nose of your saddle on your shoulder. This does not afford you as much clearance between your front wheel and the ground but you may not have an option.

Figure 7.2 Shouldering your bike in preparation to run.

I will never forget the first, and last, time I raced the season opener in Moab, Utah, in 1998. Toward the end of the loop there is a huge portage, where you have to get off your bike and carry it up a steep and rocky hiking trail. Although I had been warned ahead of time, I can still picture riding up towards it and looking up to see what looked like an ant trail of people climbing this wall with bikes on their backs (see figure 7.3). I dismounted and swung my saddle onto my shoulder. After having my front wheel hit several obstacles and voicing my opinion of the trail aloud, one of my fellow racers, Abby Paulsen, told me how to carry the bike on my back by having one hand on the saddle and one on the stem. Although this was a better position to ensure the wheels wouldn't hit any obstacles, it didn't stop me from complaining. Next time I will take a sherpa!

Figure 7.3 Carrying your bike on your back can help you avoid obstacles but it can also be cumbersome.

Now comes the tricky part—remounting your bike. Start by grabbing the bar with your left hand and grasping the middle of the down tube with your right hand. Slide the bike off your shoulder, gently placing it on the ground. Get your right hand back on the bars and in the same motion jump off of the left foot, swinging your right leg over the rear wheel. Don't jump straight up for this technique, but make it more of a rocking motion (see figure 7.4a-c). You should be jumping off the left foot and swinging your right leg over the rear wheel and rocking it forward. Get just enough height so that your rear clears your saddle. Once the right leg clears the rear wheel, land smoothly on the right inner thigh using the rocking motion, going from landing on the front of your right thigh and rocking back on to your rear. Find the pedals, clip in as quickly as possible, and you are on your way.

a

b

c

Figure 7.4 Practice riding up to an obstacle just before stopping to dismount and lifting your bike over.

CYCLO-CROSS SKILLS

PURPOSE

To practice mounting and dismounting.

WARM-UP

Warm up for 15-30 minutes at an easy pace.

TECHNIQUE

Find a big rock, a curb in front of your house, or set up some branches and rocks while out in a field or on a trail. Start by going fairly slowly and just swinging your less dominant leg over the saddle and back with out clipping the dominant leg out of the pedal. I swing my right leg over, as my left leg is my dominant leg. If you are not comfortable feeding your right leg through the left leg and the frame, just swing it to the outside of the left leg and begin your run in that manner. Once you have the leg swing down, work on unclipping the left foot and putting the right hand on the top tube or down tube and running with your bike.

Practice remounting your bike. Once you have done this several times, put an obstacle in the way and practice lifting your bike over and then remounting. This will force you to work on timing as well as your technique. The goal is to take as few steps as possible before you reach the obstacle. Once you have the bike lifting technique down, you may want to try shouldering the bike and running with it.

TIPS

Start in slow motion. Find someone who is adept at these skills and have them practice with you or go to a local cyclo-cross race.

THE REAR DEAL

PURPOSE

To practice mounting and dismounting.

WARM-UP

Warm up for 15-30 minutes before beginning this drill.

TECHNIQUE

Ride up to the obstacle or section of trail that is difficult or impossible to ride and practice dismounting, running, and remounting (see Cyclo-Cross Skills).

TIPS

If you are riding with a friend, have them try riding the difficult section while you run it. You will be amazed at how fast it can be to run once you have the technique down.

RUNNING VERSUS RIDING

Truly the hardest part about running with your bike is making the decision about whether to run or to ride. It is optimal to make that decision on your own without the circumstances making it for you. Meaning, it is better to get off and run instead of crashing and being forced to run. With that said, the two real reasons to run are: when it is very likely that you will crash when you try to ride a challenging section of the trail and when it is obviously faster to run.

When preriding a course, I look at whether the technical sections are ridable or should be run. When I come up on a technical section, I look to see what the possible lines are; I may then watch a few people ride the sections, and then I will try it. My rule of thumb is, if I crash while trying to ride it 50 percent or more, I will run it on race day. For example, at the World Cup race in Sorrento, Italy, in 2000, a section of the course had a technical right-hand turn with a drop-off at the end. You had to come into the turn slowly to set up for the drop-off correctly. If you went too slowly, you crashed before you got to the drop and if you went too quickly, you would go flying off the steep end of the drop and crash. I watched several people ride as well as crash before I attempted it. I managed to ride one time out of three, and with those odds I made the decision to run it during the race. I had also heard that one of my fellow racers landed in the hospital while trying to ride this section. I finished that race in seventh place, and running that section didn't slow me down a bit.

The other time that you may find it is better to run is when it is obviously faster. In one of the World Cup races in Canmore, Canada, in 1999, the course had a 1,000-foot section of the course that was a steep, technical climb with roots and loose rocks. If you were tired or picked the wrong line, you would have difficulty riding the whole climb. Being a steadfast climber, I was determined to ride this section. However, I heard in the men's race that one of the top guys would get off and run with his bike every time, passing most of his competitors.

The best way to determine whether it is faster to ride or run is either to time yourself or practice with a team mate. If you are riding on your own, first ride the section and then run it and see what the difference is in time. Or, if you have a teammate around, have them ride while you run and see who makes it through the section faster.

If you are not able to preride a course, at least try to go and look at the sketchy technical sections to determine whether you can ride them. If you arrive to the venue with no time to look at any parts of the course, I suggest you run any sections that you don't have confidence in riding. I may have become conservative in my old age, but I would rather make it to the finish than try something I have a good chance of crashing on. I, like most of us, am not fond of hospitals.

RUN WITH IT, BABY!

Melissa Thomas

© Courtesy of Rob Karman

"During a race the main objective is to get around the course as fast as possible without crashing. When people crash it often causes them to slow down, become frustrated, or lose their confidence in their riding ability. In the worst-case scenario, they hurt themselves or their bike. When approaching a section that is at or above your abilities, the best strategy is to learn how to get on and off your bike quickly and run it. Chances are, if someone is in front of you they will either not make the section and fall off their bike causing you to crash, or you'll have to wait until they untangle themselves and continue. If you know a technical section is approaching and you doubt your ability to clear it, then dismount quickly and run it. Often times, running a section is quicker than riding it, especially if you learn how to do a cyclo-cross dismount and remount. Once during a race in Mount Snow, Travis Brown sprinted by me and several other women carrying his bike while we were trying to ride a technical section."

PART II

Leaving Your Competition in the Dust

EIGHT

Setting Your Performance Timetable

© Courtesy of Rob Karman

When establishing your performance timetable, you first need to write down your racing schedule. After you have determined what races you will do, highlight the ones most important to you, such as the qualifiers for the World Championships. Let's call the most important races your *peak* races. This chapter will help you to construct a realistic training plan to build around your peak races. You will learn a comprehensive way to set up a training schedule going from a yearly plan to monthly and down to daily through macro-, meso-, and microcycles for training and competition. Keep in mind that everyone is unique and therefore you may need to tweak the information in this chapter to make it work best for you.

MACROCYCLES

Once you have set your goals for the year, you will be able to plan your training season. Generally the annual training season for cyclists goes from November until September of the following year. As you will see in the coming sections, this training season includes everything from endurance training to racing, with a month off in October to regroup and rest. This span of time is called a macrocycle. The macrocycle is the largest unit in the training plan and consists of a block of time spanning from 1 to 4 years.

You can set up your macrocycle in several ways. One very popular and straightforward way is to split the year up in to four separate phases: preparation, specialization, competition, and transition/recovery (see table 8.1).

I set up my macrocycle in a similar fashion but I break up my specialization phase and have athletes work on specific energy systems. Because most riders want numbers to go by, I will include a general time line for you. These times are not set in stone, so don't hold me or yourself to a strict schedule.

Preparation Phase
The preparation phase is a good time to get into the groove. Take long, slow rides, try some cross training, and begin to build up your strength as you work your way from recovery back into training mode.

2 to 5 months before your first peak

Objective: to build endurance and pedal stroke

- Long, slow rides
- Pedal stroke drills
- Weight training

Table 8.1   Macrocycle Phases

	Preparation/ foundation	Specialization	Competition	Transition/ recovery
Objective	To establish a training foundation	To develop cycling-specific performance capabilities	To approach performance capability through progressively increased competition or intensity	To significantly reduce training volume and intensity to allow for physical and psychological recovery in anticipation of the next preparation phase
Characteristics	• Progressive volume increases throughout this phase from moderate to high • Low to medium intensity • Emphasis on developing general physical performance • Weight training • Speed • Flexibility or stretching • Maintaining and refining technique	• Continuous volume increase through the middle of the phase • Volume decreases from the middle of the phase to the end of the phase • Emphasis on developing cycling-specific fitness through individualized training • Lactate threshold/tempo • $\dot{V}O_2$ • Sprints • Developing new skills • Increase in competence of old skills	• Moderate volume • Moderate to high intensity • Maintained conditioning • Emphasis on refining cycling-specific activities • Time trialing • Sprinting • Attacking • Climbing • Descending • Using tactics and strategies • Peaking	• Medical evaluation • Low to moderate volume • Low intensity • Introducing cross-training activities • Reviewing the season • Training compliance and effectiveness • Race performances • Planning for next season

Specialization Phase I: Lactate Threshold

Specializing means working at a higher pace, performing harder intervals, and cutting back slightly on the hours of training. This is the phase in which you begin to train your body to tolerate and clear lactic acid, and work your phosphocreatine (PC) system so your body becomes more efficient at short burst intervals.

1 to 2 months before your first peak

Objective: to work on lactic acid tolerance and clearing

• Building lactate threshold/tempo

- Clearing lactic acid
- Short-burst intervals

Specialization Phase II: $\dot{V}O_2$

The second phase of specialization focuses on maximum effort ($\dot{V}O_2$ max) intervals. You also want to work on strengthening your technical skills, eliminating weaknesses, and practicing your starts.

1 week to 6 weeks before your first peak

Objective: high intensity training and skills training

- $\dot{V}O_2$ or maximum effort intervals
- Working on weaknesses
- Improving technical skills
- Training races
- Practicing starts
- Tapering for the big race

Competition Phase

In the competition phase the goal is to stay fresh for race days by tapering your training.

3 to 4 months of peak racing season

Objective: to maintain fitness and continue to hone skills

- Race!
- Rebuilding for second and third peak
- Honing skills
- Working on weaknesses

Transition/Recovery Phase

Use the transition and recovery phase to do exactly what the name implies. Take some time out, try some new or different activities, and recover physically and mentally for the next racing season.

1 to 3 months during the off-season

Objective: to mentally and physically take a break

- Cross-training
- Weight training
- Sitting on the couch
- Daydreaming
- Going to the movies
- Riding for fun

It's important to taper your training so you're fresh for the race.

Now that you have the basics for making up your training year, get out your calendar and mark it up. First, put down when your peak races are and start working backward. When choosing your peak races, realize you can only peak 2 to 3 times in a year. A seasoned racer can hold their peak for up to 2 weeks, so if you have two important races back to back or on consecutive weekends, plan to peak for both. Once you have planned your racing calendar, work backward from the first peak race and plug in when you will be doing each phase.

Let me give you an example. Rider A is a professional racer whose goal is to go to the World Championships. To get invited, she needs to place in the top 5 in a World Cup race. The races she does best at are in Canada in June as well as in Belgium in July and therefore we will plan on her peaking for those races as well as for the World Championships in September (see table 8.2).

Rider B is an expert racer who works full time and therefore cannot do all of the racing he would like. His goals are to place in the top 3 overall in

Table 8.2   Racing Schedule Rider A

Month	Phase	Activity
October	Recovery	• Cross training (hiking or running)
November	Recovery/transition	• Begin riding • Weight training
December	Transition	• Long easy rides (3-4 hours) • Work on pedal stroke
January	Transition	• Long easy rides (4-5 hours) • Work on pedal stroke
February	Specialization I	• Begin lactate threshold (LT) intervals.
March	Specialization I/II	• Continue LT intervals and begin $\dot{V}O_2$ intervals
April	Specialization II	• Continue $\dot{V}O_2$ intervals and work on technical skills
May	Competition	• Racing
June	Peak	• June 2: World Cup Race • June 9: World Cup Race
July	Peak	• July 30: World Cup Race
August	Specialization I/II	• Rebuild for World Championships
September	Peak	• Sept 5: World Championships

his local race series and place in the top 10 in the two national races he is able to attend. To place top 3 overall, he needs to place in the top 5 in all seven of the races in the series or place in the top 3 in at least three of the races. Because he cannot attend all seven of the races, he is hoping to place in the top 3 in the three races that are near him and maybe race two other races in the series. His peak races will then be the two nationals, which are in July and August, the two local races near him, which are in May and June, and the final local race, which is also in August. See table 8.3. Every racer's schedule is different. A high-level racer will ride and race more months in the year and have less time off.

Lastly, the training schedule becomes cloudier when determining what to do in between your second and third peak race. In a perfect world, the peak races will be spaced at least 4 weeks from each other to give you enough time to rest and ramp up again. If your peak races are closer together than 4 weeks, you will have to punt: Either get a coach to tell you what to do or break up the time you have in between each peak to a mini rest and ramp week.

Table 8.3   Racing Schedule Rider B

Month	Phase	Activity
October	Recovery	• Cross training (hiking, yoga)
November	Recovery	• Cross training (skating, skiing)
December	Transition	• Long easy rides (3-4 hours) • Pedal stroke drills
January	Transition	• Long easy rides (4-5 hours) • Pedal stroke drills
February	Specialization I	• Begin lactate threshold intervals
March	Specialization I/II	• Continue lactate threshold intervals and start $\dot{V}O_2$ intervals
April	Specialization II	• Continue $\dot{V}O_2$ intervals • Work on technical skills
May	Competition	• Peak May 30—Local race
June	Competition	• Peak June 7—Local race
July	Competition	• Peak July 4—National race
August	Competition	• Peak August 1—Final local race • Peak August 22—National race
September	Recovery	• Easy month (do whatever you enjoy)

MESOCYCLES

Now you need to further break the training phases down in to smaller units. These units are called mesocycles and can be anywhere from 3 to 9 weeks long. I use a 4-week cycle because it is easy to follow and gives the athlete a rest week every fourth week of training. Every coach or athlete needs to determine what works best for them and go with it.

Mesocycles are generally built around increasing your training load or honing specific skills. A training load can be hours or miles on the bike, intensity of the rides, frequency or number of rides in a week, or simply working on specific technical skills. Many times an athlete may be working on more than one aspect of training in a mesocycle. For instance, a 4-week training cycle in the preparation phase of training will focus on increasing the hours on the bike each consecutive week as well as working on smoothing out pedal stroke.

Week 1: 8 hours training
Week 2: 10 hours training

Week 3: 12 hours training

Week 4: 6 hours training

See table 8.4 for Rider A's schedule.

Table 8.4 Rider A's $\dot{V}O_2$ schedule

Week	Hours	Activity
Week 1	9	$\dot{V}O_2$ intervals (2 days) = 5.5 hrs. Technical skills (1 day) = 2 hrs. Starts (1 day) = 1.5 hrs.
Week 2	10	$\dot{V}O_2$ pt intervals (2 days) = 6.5 hrs. Technical skills (1day) = 2 hrs. Starts (1 day) = 1.5 hrs.
Week 3	11	$\dot{V}O_2$ intervals (2 days) = 7 hrs. Technical skills (1 day) = 2.5 hours. Starts (1 day) = 1.5 hrs.
Week 4	7	$\dot{V}O_2$ intervals (1 day) = 2.5 hrs. Technical skills (1 day) = 2 hrs. Starts (1 day) = 1.5 hr. ride. 1 easy spin = 1 hr.

The key to each mesocycle is to push you to your limit, or make you *overreach,* the week before rest week. So whether you decide to use a 4-week or a 6-week ramp-up schedule, make sure that you are working your hardest on the week before rest week. But don't work so hard that you become *overtrained.* See page 166 for a discussion on overreaching versus overtraining.

MICROCYCLES

The next smallest training unit is the microcycle. Microcycles are most commonly broken up in to 7-day cycles that are centered around weekend competitions. Each day of a microcycle is designated for a specific workload depending on the phase of training. The volume, intensity, and frequency of the workload will vary each day depending on the week of training you are in. Each microcycle will also have changes in workload depending on your tolerance and weekly work or school schedule. For example, a week in the preparation phase is

Monday: easy spin/off

Tuesday: 1-hour ride working on leg drills

Wednesday: weight training

Thursday: long slow ride of 2.0 hours

Friday: weight training

Saturday: long slow ride of 3.0 hours

Sunday: fun ride or cross-training activity for 2 to 3 hours

I will generally ramp up an athlete's schedule throughout the week, with the hardest rides on the weekend. Because many athletes work, they have more time on the weekends to put into riding. They are also most likely to be tired on Monday, so it is a good rest day. I also don't like to have too many hard days in a row (2 to 3 at the most) to avoid burnout. Variations obviously exist to all of these cycles depending on time, ability level, and stage of racing and riding, so find what riding schedule works best for your week and go with it.

Be aware that no two people are alike and therefore everyone's schedule should be different. Don't use a cookie-cutter approach or follow what someone else is doing. Find what works for you and stick with it.

NINE

Monitoring Your Progress

Now that you have made your calendar for the year, outlining when you will be racing, your peak races, and your phases of training, in this chapter I will educate you on how to monitor your training. In order to do this in a measurable way, I will tell you how to use a heart rate monitor and the wattage meter or the rate of perceived exertion (RPE) method. These measurements enable you to track your progress and determine how hard you need to be riding and if you are gaining in strenths.

MEASURING YOUR EFFORT WITH RPE

The rating of perceived exertion (RPE) scale is a subjective method by which to rate the difficulty of your effort. It is primarily used for testing purposes but can also be used as a training tool. The RPE scale can be numbered from either 1 to 10 or 1 to 20. Again, it is subjective, so use the scale that works best for you. I like to use the 1-to-10 scale. Basically, you are either working easy, moderate, or hard; there isn't too much in between. Here is my own variation of the 1-to-10 RPE scale:

1 = sleeping

2 = very, very easy

3 = very easy

4 = easy

5 = light

6 = moderate

7 = somewhat hard

8 = hard

9 = very hard

10= very, very hard (vomiting)

As you can see, these adjectives are very subjective, so you can come up with your own descriptions.

You can use the RPE scale in place of a heart rate monitor or watt meter if you cannot afford either of these tools. However, I suggest you first use them to help pinpoint exactly at what level you should be training. Once you become familiar with how you are feeling at a specific training level, you can translate that number to a perceived exertion rating. For example, you may need to train at your lactate threshold (LT), or the point at which your body accumulates lactic acid. After doing a field test or being tested in a lab, you know your heart rate at LT is between 160 and 165 beats per minute. When you are training in the specialization phase, you will need to do intervals where your heart rate is right between 160 and 165. To be specific, you will need a heart rate monitor. After using your heart rate monitor for several weeks, you will be able to determine when your heart rate is between 160 and 165, or you are at an RPE of 7 to 8, because you are no longer able to talk while riding or your breathing is becoming labored. Once you learn to read your body at certain heart rates, you will no longer need your heart rate monitor and you can use the RPE scale to monitor your workloads. It may take several years to feel comfortable using the RPE scale instead of a more specific tool, nevertheless it can be very useful. Again, if you do not have the resources to purchase a heart rate monitor, you can use the RPE scale; it is just not as specific. To help you further, table 9.1 provides a chart that coincides training zones with heart rates and RPE. Training zones, which will be discussed next, is a method of breaking up your heart rate into ranges to help simplify your training.

Table 9.1   Zone, HR, and RPE Measurements

Zones	1	2	3	4	5
% HR max	<65%	65-72%	73-80%	84-90%	91-100%
Breathing	Can sign or whistle	Able to converse	Talking is hard	Forced breathing	Very forced breathing
RPE	Very easy	Easy	Light	Hard	Very, very hard

Adapted, by permission, from USA Cycling, Inc., 1995, *Expert level coaching manual* (Colorado Springs, CO: USA Cycling), 76.

FINDING YOUR ZONE

One fairly objective way to monitor your training is to use a heart rate (HR) monitor. I say *fairly* objective because your HR can be a less accurate gauge in certain situations, such as when dehydrated or when riding in extreme temperatures. With that said, HR monitors are still very good training tools and are reasonably affordable.

Training zones are percentages of your maximum heart rate (HRmax), or the highest heart rate that you have seen on your heart rate monitor. Don't get picky yet; I will give you some ways of testing for your HRmax in the next section, including both scientific and low-budget methods.

Several variations of zones exist. I use the USA Cycling calculations because they are concise and don't leave too much room for error. If you make things too complicated, you will not accomplish what you set out to do; you will spend more time mapping out the details than riding your bike. Here is a summary of the zones I use:

• **Zone 1:** Riding in this HR is basically used for active recovery. You can do it as a 30-minute to 1-hour ride the day after a race or hard ride. It will help increase blood flow to your muscles and therefore increase the healing process. It also helps keep legs from getting stiff.

- **Zone 2:** Riding in this zone is generally done for endurance training. It is the long, slow, early-season ride ranging from 1 to 5 or more hours. Riding in this zone will help develop the aerobic energy system. It is also said to help the body utilize fat to produce energy.

Riding in this zone helps the body develop neuromuscular pathways that in effect make you a more efficient rider. It also gives you the mental fortitude to tolerate long hours on your bike, which will help you to mentally tolerate long races.

- **Zone 3:** Riding in this zone is still considered aerobic training. You are still utilizing mostly fats as your energy source, however the body is beginning to burn carbohydrate as well. This zone can be lumped in with zone 2 as an endurance builder but is best done in a 2- to 3-hour ride. Riding in this zone will also help the body become more efficient at utilizing oxygen.

- **Zone 4:** Riding in this zone will help improve the body's ability to tolerate and clear lactic acid and is known as the lactate threshold zone. It is at this zone that the body begins burning more carbohydrate as a fuel source while continuing to utilize oxygen. Riding in this zone is done in bouts of anywhere from 5 minutes to 1 hour. It is the zone in which most mountain bike racers spend their time. Therefore, much of your training should be in and around this zone.

- **Zone 5:** Riding in this zone is generally to improve your $\dot{V}O_2$max as well as your ability to sprint. It is meant to help your body tolerate activity at a limited oxygen supply. The intervals done at this zone can vary from 8 seconds to 8 minutes in duration.

Now that you have an idea of your training zones, you can correlate these zones to your RPE. Table 9.2 provides a simple chart to help you visualize it.

Table 9.2   Zone and HR Measurements

Zone	% of max Heart Rate	Description of Training
1	< 65 %	easy riding, recovery
2	66-72%	basic endurance, aerobic capacity
3	73-80%	tempo, aerobic capacity
4	84-90%	lactate threshold
5	91-100%	$\dot{V}O_2$, sprint training, max efforts

Reprinted, by permission, from USA Cycling, Inc., *Training manual for mountain biking* (Colorado Springs, CO: USA Cycling), 6-7.

To determine your training zones, you will first need to know your maximum heart rate described in the next section.

TESTING FOR MAXIMUM HEART RATE

You can test your HR max in several ways. One of the more simple methods can be done on a bicycle while riding outside, as long as you have a bicycle computer that reads power or miles per hour: Warm up for at least 15 minutes. Then increase the difficulty of your effort every 1 minute by increasing miles per hour or power output, until you reach exhaustion. This part will probably last between 5 and 10 minutes. Once you reach that last minute where you feel you cannot go another minute, go as hard as you can for 30 seconds. The highest observed heart rate is then considered your HR max. To be as precise as possible, it is best to do this test on a bicycle ergometer or a CompuTrainer rather than do it as a field test. It will allow you to have better control when increasing resistance and time as well as allow you to keep environmental factors consistent, such as temperature and wind resistance, so that you can recreate these factors when retesting. Although this method will not give exact numbers, it is inexpensive and can more easily be done several times throughout the year to test your progress.

The most precise way of finding your HRmax is to get it tested in a physiology lab. The physiologist will use a bicycle ergometer and be able to monitor heart rate, RPE, and oxygen levels in a controlled setting. If no physiology lab exists near you and you still want the most precise measurements possible, you may want to call your local college or university to ask whether they do physiologic testing.

Sometimes I simply ask an athlete, "What is the highest number you have ever seen on your heart rate monitor?" This method is obviously not scientific or the most accurate, but I can get a general idea of an athlete's HRmax from that information. Remember, I am of the school of no frills. Don't get me wrong; I have been tested several times and I have used that information faithfully. It is always best to get exact numbers for your HRmax. However, unless you are a high-level athlete or are interested in getting exact numbers, you can get close to your HRmax using less exact methods.

The only pieces of equipment you need to train using heart rate zones are a bike and a heart rate monitor. The difficulty arises when you are trying to determine what heart rate monitor will work best for you. Polar heart rate monitors are the most well known; however, other companies, such as Cateye, make very good monitors. When purchasing a heart rate monitor, think about what functions you just can't live without. The two features that I think are most important are simply being able to see your heart rate throughout your ride and the ability to get your average heart rate for the ride or for a specific interval. It would be great to be able to set your monitor up to tell you when you are in specific heart rate zones and how much time you spent in those zones. The ultimate monitor is one that allows you to download information and store it so you can compare workouts or races. Again, in a perfect world every cyclist would have the best equipment possible and know how to use it. As you know, the world is far from perfect and having all of the bells and whistles will not guarantee you a spot on the Olympic team. Some of us only used a heart rate monitor occasionally and mostly had a watch strapped on to our bars.

DETERMINING YOUR POWER AND $\dot{V}O_2$MAX

One of the newest tools used to monitor training levels is a power meter. Power is defined as the amount of energy generated per unit of time. A power meter measures how much energy (in watts) is transferred onto the pedals every second. A few different types of power meters are currently on the market—one is the Power Tap and another is the SRM. Polar has also recently come out with a tool for measuring your power output while on the bike.

Measuring power output is currently the most efficient way of measuring your intensity while on the bike. Although a heart rate monitor is still the most widely used and has been trusted longer, a power meter is rapidly becoming the tool of choice. The reason a power meter is more effective than a heart rate monitor is that heart rate can fluctuate with changes in core (or internal body) temperature. Heart rate can also fluctuate with the change in outside temperature as well as with dehydration. Finally, it can take several seconds for a heart rate monitor to accurately read a change in riding intensity. Conversely, the amount of power a cyclist is generating remains constant with the change in environment whether it be the cyclist's core temperature or external conditions. If a cyclist is pushing 300 watts, it will not change whether they are going uphill, riding into the wind, or have not eaten a good breakfast. The factors that may change in these different circumstances are how fast the cyclist is going or how they are feeling, but 300 watts is 300 watts.

For example, consider an athlete who was tested to determine his lactate threshold. He was then given his heart rate and watts as well as his RPE level at lactate threshold. His heart rate was between 165 and 170, his power output was 300 watts, and his RPE was 8. Given this information the athlete can then go out and train at lactate threshold using any or all of these methods. Say he goes out to do a training session where he needs to stay at lactate threshold for 15 minutes. It is a very hot day, with temperatures in the hundreds. While riding in what he thinks is lactate threshold, he notices that his heart rate is at 175 but his power output shows 300 watts. His heart rate is 10 beats higher because of the heat, but he is still most likely riding at his lactate threshold.

To use a power meter effectively, you must be tested to determine your wattage range when riding in each energy system. The two most crucial energy systems to test for are lactate threshold and $\dot{V}O_2$max. Once you have determined your power output, you can then train at these levels to become more efficient.

The previous section mentioned several methods for determining HRmax. To determine power output by using the previous tests, you need to note your wattage while at a given heart rate. For example, if you are doing the field test to determine your HRmax while on a CompuTrainer, you can also get a reading for your power output. In a ramp test for HRmax, the tester increases the resistance by 25 watts every minute. Once the athlete is unable to continue pedaling the tester takes the readings for both heart rate and power output. The highest heart rate reading is said to be HRmax. The highest power output reading is then the power output at HRmax.

Once you get your HRmax, you can calculate your $\dot{V}O_2$max. I tend to use these two measurements interchangeably because many of us will reach our $\dot{V}O_2$max close to the same time we reach our HRmax. However, they are not the same. $\dot{V}O_2$max is the maximum amount of oxygen uptake, or the ability of the body to utilize oxygen and deliver it to the working muscles to produce energy. Therefore, an athlete generally reaches their $\dot{V}O_2$max before seeing their HRmax. This will be discussed further in the chapter on $\dot{V}O_2$max. In order to get a true reading of ones $\dot{V}O_2$max, and your heart rate and power output at $\dot{V}O_2$max, you need to be tested in a laboratory with the capability of monitoring your oxygen uptake.

Before you begin testing you should have some background on lactate threshold. Lactate, or lactic acid, is produced when the body is unable to supply all of its energy needs by using oxygen. Once your body reaches a certain level of lactate accumulation it will no longer be able to hold its intensity because of the buildup of lactate in the muscles. The point at which the body begins to slow down because of lactate accumulation in the muscles is called lactate threshold (LT) and is currently the level at which most athletes train. For more information on lactate threshold, see page 153.

To get a ballpark reading of LT, I like to use is a time trial test. People use various distances or time limits for this field test. I do a simple 10-

mile time trial, which works out well when going from Boulder to Lyons on Highway 36. Get a good warm-up of at least 20 minutes and then go as hard as you can for 10 miles. During that time you will be monitoring several factors, two of which should be your average heart rate and average power. Both of these measurements are a benchmark for your lactate threshold and should be used in the future when doing LT intervals. The other factors that you should monitor are amount of wind, time of day, temperature, and possibly when and what you ate last. These factors are all important to re-create when doing a retest later in the season.

To train at $\dot{V}O_2$max and lactate threshold while using your power meter, you need to monitor your wattage while performing specific intervals. For example, if you are working on increasing your lactate threshold and you have found your power output at LT to be between 240 and 250 watts, you need to do intervals within those parameters. I will go over more specific intervals in chapter 10.

The best time to test your LT or $\dot{V}O_2$max is toward the end of the endurance phase of training. It is important to have some fitness and miles in your legs before testing because testing can be stressful on the body. If you are concerned about staying below your lactate threshold when in the endurance phase, you should have a lactate threshold test done, just to make sure you are at the desired level.

If you have access to a testing facility or you want to become more efficient at your own field testing, you may want to do an LT test before you start the endurance phase. It will also give you an idea of your current lactate threshold and what your heart rate and power should be when riding in the endurance phase.

The most important time to test is just before you start your LT intervals. In the endurance phase you should be able to keep a slow pace without having to watch your heart rate; however, once you reach the specialization phases, you need to more closely monitor your heart rate and power output. So, test yourself to make sure you are using the correct numbers for heart rate and power output.

As I have mentioned previously in this chapter, your lactate threshold will change with training. Therefore, it is to your advantage to test yourself before the specialization phase as well as every 4 to 6 weeks leading up to the competition phase. By doing so you will ensure that you are becoming more efficient with lactate tolerance and clearing. You should also adjust the heart rate and power output at which you are training as your body becomes more efficient.

TEN

Refining Your Training Schedule

Now that you have your yearly schedule mapped out and you know what types of training tools you will use as well as when to be tested and how, it is time to start training. In this chapter you will learn about the four phases of training—preparation, specialization (I and II), competition, and transition and recovery along with the benefits of overreaching and the dangers of overtraining.

It is important to work on your technical skills and any weaknesses that you may have. This is also a good time to take part in some training races as well as practice your starts. The start of a mountain bike race will determine how you will finish. If you don't have a good start, you will have only a slim chance of making the top 10. Doing a few practice races in your area is a good idea. This will give you some feedback on how your training is going and most likely push you to train harder.

PREPARATION PHASE

The start of your training year, or early season, begins with your base training or preparation phase. This means long, slow riding, keeping your heart rate down, riding on road bikes, group rides, building your endurance, training your diet, practicing your pedal stroke by doing some drill work, and cross training.

Taking Long Slow Rides

The true purpose of the long slow rides (LSR) is to increase your body's ability to tolerate sitting on the bike as well as to increase your body's fat-burning capability. Most coaches agree that the early season is the best time to build endurance. If you question your training at all, you should find another coach or training book, because if you do not believe that what you are doing will help, it won't!

The only way you will tolerate racing long hours on your bike, both mentally and physically, is to spend long hours on your bike. I generally say that your long rides should be one-fourth to one-third longer than your longest race. So, if your longest race is 3 hours, you better be able to tolerate 3.75 to 4 hours on the bike. This does not hold true for riders who are planning to do ultra-distance or 24-hour races. That's a different form of torture that will not be covered in this book.

When you do long slow rides, your body becomes more efficient at taking up oxygen, pumping it through your system, and getting it to the muscles. Your body also learns to fire the muscles more efficiently and use those muscles that need to be working. It is also said that at this intensity of training, your body primarily uses fat as an energy source and therefore learns to use it more efficiently. I don't know that this has been scientifically proven but let me tell you, it is a good motivator. There is also a huge mental component to cycling and racing. People often have problems in riding or racing for an extended period. By doing these long rides, you will know without a doubt that you can tolerate being on the bike for 3, 4, or even 5 hours and therefore will have no problem with a 2.5-hour race.

When I started mountain bike racing I was racing for 1 to 1.5 hours at a time. I had no problem racing for that amount of time because that was the average amount of time I would spend on my bike. Once I moved up to the expert and pro class, all hell broke loose. I was then expected to be hammering up to 2.5 hours. I would go out hard and then perish at about the 1.5-hour mark because that is what I was used to and could tolerate. I then got a coach (hint, hint) who put me on a schedule where I would ride for 4 to 5 hours on a hard week. That does not mean by the next season I was able to race my heart out for 2.5 hours, but I knew that I could tolerate that distance without hitting a wall. It took me several years of training before I could race all out for 2.5 hours.

Gauging Heart Rate

Your heart rate for a long slow ride should be between 66 and 72 percent of your maximal heart rate. Because you have already calculated your maximum, you can come up with the appropriate numbers. For example, if you have found through testing that your maximal heart rate is 190, you will want to stay below 140 beats per minute while doing your endurance riding. Or, by looking at the chart in chapter 9, you will know that you should be able to have a conversation and your rating of perceived exertion should be "easy." If you are using a power meter, you should disconnect it, or make sure that you are staying below 72 percent of your maximal power output. If your power output at maximal heart rate was 350 watts, when doing long easy rides your power should be below 250 watts. During this phase I tell people not to use their heart rate monitors or power meters. You can do a few of the early rides with a heart rate monitor or power meter to make sure you are not going above the level you need to be at; otherwise just take it easy and enjoy the scenery.

Hitting the Road

All of the early-season riding should be done on a road bike. If you don't own a road bike you should purchase a pair of slick tires so that you can ride your mountain bike on the road with less resistance. Riding a road bike to do long slow hours is less taxing on your body. This is not the time to be overstressing your body. Riding your mountain bike on the road is a great idea, especially if you have slicks on, because it will get you comfortable on the bike you will be racing. The disadvantage is that the mountain bike is heavier and less aerodynamic, so it will slow you down.

Group riding is a great way to get in a long slow ride without getting too bored. You have people to talk to and wheels to sit on in order to get a draft. The problem with group rides is that the rest of the group may ride harder than you need to go. In general, when you get a group of cyclists together, there is a tendency to push one another. This will mean that the pace is higher than it needs to be for that time of year. I think one or maybe two group rides a week during this time of year are fine. The best plan is to find a group that is going at your pace. As a mountain bike racer, you should do some of the long rides on your own. In a race, you will spend some time with no other racers in your sight, so you'll want to get used to riding on your own.

Building Endurance

You do not want to go out on a 5-hour ride if the longest ride you have ever done is 2 hours. Your body will rebel and you may end up with tendinitis or bursitis and have to take time off from riding your bike. In any type of training you do, you'll want to slowly ramp up to give your body time to adapt. You need to take into account how long your rides were the previous year and even the year before that to determine what you can tolerate. I would suggest increasing your time by 1 to 1.5 hours each year. For example, if your longest ride the previous year was 2 hours, your longest ride this year should 3 to 3.5 hours. When building your endurance using the 4-week ramp-up, the weeks should look something like this:

Week 1: Two rides of 2.0 hours each

Week 2: Two rides of 2.5 hours each

Week 3: Two rides of 3.0 hours each

Week 4: Two rides of 1.5 hours each

You will be doing other rides in these weeks, but this gives you an idea of how to increase your endurance rides.

Rest is the most important part of training. Rest does not mean going to work, playing with the kids, or going shopping. Rest means lying on the couch or in bed with your legs up. Just like stretching, rest is highly overlooked. As a racer, you will never get stronger unless you allow your body some serious rest. Resting is not something that we all have the luxury of doing, so you'd better build it into your riding schedule.

It is said that you need to rest as many hours as you train. This does not include the hours you sleep at night; this is *in addition* to the hours you sleep at night. But I wouldn't say that if you do a 5-hour ride, you'd need to take a 5-hour nap. I would suggest that any time you do a ride of 2 to 3 hours, you should give yourself at least 30 minutes of downtime during the day. For any ride longer than 3 hours, you should give yourself 1 to 2 hours a day with your legs up. Consider this training time. If you do not rest, your body will not be able to tolerate the ride the next day or you will not continue to make gains in your training. The last little tidbit on resting: When you sleep your body secretes a hormone that helps your muscles to heal. So, make sure you get a good amount of sleep at night (8 to 9 hours), and take a nap or at least put your legs up during the day on those long training days.

Training Your Diet

The preparation phase is also a good time to get into the habit of training your diet by eating and drinking well. If you are going to do a ride over 1.5 hours, make sure you are well hydrated. Not only should you drink water, but you should also drink a beverage that replaces carbohydrate and electrolytes. This is a good time to experiment with drink mixes and find one that you like and one that your body will tolerate. The bottom line is that if you don't like the taste of the drink mix, you won't drink it. I can remember seeing one of my fellow racers off her bike on the side of the trail getting sick during a race because her body was not tolerating the drink mix she used.

I often have my athletes practice drinking during their rides. Set your watch to beep every 15-20 minutes and take a good swig every time it goes off. Or every time you go by a sign on the road, take a drink. It doesn't matter what type of signal you use to motivate yourself to drink, but you should get in the habit of drinking at least one water bottle for every hour that you ride.

A good diet is important when you're training and riding. You may want to talk with a nutritionist, who can give you an idea of what will work for you. You should get adequate protein and fat in your diet. Carbohydrate is the basic fuel we use to propel us forward on our bikes, but our bodies also require protein and fat for muscle repair and hormone production. Try to have protein and fat in every meal. Make sure it is high-quality fat and protein (such as nuts, vegetable oils, soy products, dairy, and lean meats), not fat and protein from fast food. You probably know what is good for you, but you might not practice good eating habits. If you have limited time to make good meals or to eat snacks, find a drink mix that contains carbohydrate, protein, and fat, and have that as your snack. Plenty of good meal-replacement bars are also on the market. Because many of these products contain preservatives and artificial ingredients, they aren't as good for you as actual meals, but they are better than greasy fast food or no food at all.

Practicing Your Pedal Stroke

During the preparation phase, you also want to get started on your pedal stroke drills. I have gone into depth about pedal stroke drills in chapter 2, so go back and get familiar with them. I generally start people off with single-leg drills and work in some high-cadence drills after the first 4-6 weeks of the preparation phase. I have my athletes continue with some form of pedal stroke drills up until the competition phase, tapering off of the single-leg drills and high-cadence drills and going into strength and endurance drills in the specialization phase. Don't scrimp on the pedal stroke drills, they will help in all aspects of you training.

Cross Training

During the preparation phase you should also be doing some weight training. Sign up at a gym and have one of the trainers get you in to a weight training program that is geared around cycling. As with everything, some trainers are very knowledgeable and some are not. The most important thing is to get a well rounded strength program as this will help keep you from getting injured when you begin doing harder efforts on the bike.

SPECIALIZATION PHASE I

After having trained for 6 to 12 weeks in the preparation phase, it is time to start specializing—working at a higher pace, performing harder intervals, and cutting back slightly on training hours. In this phase you begin to train the body to tolerate lactic acid and educate it on how to clear lactic acid. Specialization phase I is also the time to start working on short-burst intervals or phosphocreatine (PC) jumps. The next section explains the how and why of lactic acid and lactate threshold and will give you specific intervals to perform.

Defining Lactic Acid and Lactate Threshold

When carbohydrates are broken down in the absence of oxygen to produce energy (ATP), one of the end products is lactic acid. So when you go from a slow or endurance pace of riding (where your body is utilizing oxygen) to a higher pace (where your body is not getting as much oxygen), you begin to accumulate lactic acid.

"The increase in lactic acid is associated with a proportionate increase in the production of hydrogen ions, which make the environment of your muscle cells more acidic. This [change in chemistry] results in temporary muscle fatigue; the increased hydrogen ion concentration has been shown to limit the force-generating capacity of the muscle and decrease the rate of ATP production."

In other words, once the muscles accumulate a lot of lactic acid, clearing it out of the muscles will require oxygen. So, you will need to slow down enough that the muscles begin to utilize oxygen to produce energy. During a mountain bike race, a rider will spend a lot of time around lactate threshold, so training the body to tolerate lactic acid is very important. First you need to determine your lactate threshold, either by using a field test or by getting tested in a laboratory. These tests are discussed on page 144. Once you know your lactic acid threshold, you can train the body to tolerate lactic acid by riding at or just below that level. This training requires performing intervals ranging from 5 to 60 minutes long, keeping your heart rate at or below your lactate threshold, with repetitions from 1 to 5 times depending on the time of your interval. For example, if your lactate threshold is at a heart rate of 160 beats per minute, you should begin your intervals of 4×5 minutes, with a 3- to 5-minute easy spin in between, keeping your heart rate below 160 beats per minute. From there you should build up your time until you can sustain this intensity for 30 to 60 minutes at a time. You should take equal or half as much time off in between each bout. The longest lactate threshold intervals I worked up to were 3×30 minutes long with a 20-minute easy spin in between each. With that said, don't kill yourself with these intervals. Work up slowly during this phase as well as throughout your training career to ensure that you don't burn out before your time. A sample month building lactate tolerance would look like this:

> Week 1: LT intervals of 3×10 minutes, with a 10-minute easy spin in between each; 2 times a week in a 1.5-hour ride
>
> Week 2: LT intervals of 4×10 minutes, with a 10-minute easy spin in between each; 2 times a week in a 2.0-hour ride
>
> Week 3: LT intervals of 3×15 minutes, with a 10-minute easy spin in between each; 2 times a week in a 2.5-hour ride
>
> Week 4: LT intervals of 2×10 minutes, with a 10-minute easy spin in between each; 2 times a week in a 1-hour ride

Clearing Lactic Acid

To train your body to clear lactic acid, you need to build it up first. The idea is to ride short durations at an intensity where your body is building lactic acid and then come down below that level so that your body will then clear it out. You can do it in two ways: First, you can ride at short intervals from 60 to 90 seconds at a time, then ride below LT or at an easy pace for twice the duration of the intervals. For example, you may want to do 4×1-minute intervals with a 2-minute easy spin in between each. Second, you can gradually work up to an intensity at which your body is accumulating lactic acid and then ride easy or below LT for a prescribed period. The difference between these intervals and the lactate tolerance intervals is that with lactate tolerance intervals, you are staying at or below your lactate threshold. With lactate clearing intervals you are going over your lactate threshold and then coming back down below it to clear the lactic acid. For example, I like to have my riders do hill repeats: riding for 4 minutes below LT than sprinting for 1 minute, then going back to below LT for 4 minutes, and so on. You can do it 2 to 4 times before taking a 20-minute easy spin in between. Again, you can change the time and number of intervals around depending on how fit you are and how many years you have been training (see table 10.1).

Because your body becomes more efficient at tolerating and clearing lactic acid, it is a good idea to retest your lactate threshold after 4 to 6 weeks of performing intervals. It will also determine whether your body is adapting and actually becoming more efficient. Again, it is more accurate to be tested in a physiology lab, you may not be able to afford multiple tests. In this case, becoming more effective at performing field tests is a good plan. Use the test as one of your interval sessions because the tests are just as taxing.

Table 10.1 Monthly Schedule for Clearing Lactic Acid

Week	Activity
1	• 1 day with LC intervals of 5×1 minute with a 2-minute easy spin in between each; should be a 1-1.5 hour ride • 1 day with LC intervals of 2×10 minutes, 4.5 minutes below LT and 30-second sprint, then back to below LT for 4.5 minutes and sprint for 30 seconds, with a 10-minute easy spin in between each interval; should be a 1.5-hour ride
2	• 1 day with LC intervals of 6×1 minute, with a 2-minute easy spin in between each interval; should be a 1.5-hour ride • 1 day with LC intervals of 3×10 minutes, 4.5 minutes below LT and 30-second sprint, with a 10-minute easy spin in between each interval; should be a 2.0-hour ride
3	• 1 day with LC intervals of 6×1 minute, with a 2-minute easy spin in between each interval; should be a 1.5- to 2.0-hour ride • 1 day with LC intervals of 4×10 minutes, 4.5 minutes below LT and a 30-second sprint, with a 10-minute easy spin in between each interval; should be a 2.5-hour ride
4	• 1 day with LC intervals of 4×1 minute, with a 2-minute easy spin in between each interval; should be a 1-hour ride • 1 day with LC intervals of 4×5 minutes, with 4.5 minutes below LT and sprint for 30 seconds and a 5-minute easy spin in between each interval; should be a 1.5-hour ride

Training the Phosphocreatine System

While working on increasing their lactate threshold, I have my athletes also work on the phosphocreatine (PC) system, which your body uses to produce adenosine triphosphate (ATP), or energy. Your body breaks down ATP molecules in the absence of oxygen to produce energy. This anaerobic system is only utilized in short bursts of up to 8 seconds in duration. It is utilized during mountain biking in the start of a race, when sprinting for the single track sections or to get away from another rider, and when in a sprint finish. Depending on individual muscle makeup, a rider may either be good at sprinting or not. However, an athlete can become more adept at sprinting by training the PC system.

How do you train your body to become more efficient at utilizing phosophocreatine? By performing intervals, of course. The more you have your body use this energy system, the more it will learn how to use it appropriately. It is also a good idea to visualize what you will be using these intervals for, while you perform them. For example, if you think about sprinting past someone on to a single track section while you are performing these intervals, it will help you to work on your tactics as well as your technique at the same time. It will also make you work a little harder at the intervals. With this said, the intervals I have my athletes work on are anywhere from 5 to 8 intervals of 8-second sprints with a 2-minute easy spin in between each interval. A 4-week ramp-up would look like this

Week 1: 6×8-second intervals with a 2-minute easy spin in between each interval

Week 2: 7×8-second intervals with a 2-minute easy spin in between each interval

Week 3: 8×8-second intervals with a 2-minute easy spin in between each interval

Week 4: (rest week): 5×8-second intervals with a 2-minute easy spin in between each interval

Keep in mind that you should always do a good 15- to 20-minute warm-up before performing these intervals. So the next question is how long can it last and do I use a mountain bike or a road bike?

• Duration. Neal Henderson, physiologist at the Boulder Center for Sports Medicine, told me that your body can actually lose its ability to tolerate and clear lactic acid in a span of around 4 weeks. Once you stop doing intervals or riding and racing around your lactate threshold, your body stops producing the enzymes that break down the lactic acid. With this said, it is important to continue to remind your body how to tolerate and clear lactic acid once you have the system running well. Continue to do at least 1 day a week of LT or LC intervals up until you begin racing.

Once you start racing, you will be working both the lactate tolerance and lactate clearing systems during the race.

- Mountain or road bike. The type of bike and terrain you choose for these intervals will depend on the time of season you will perform them. When beginning to work on lactate threshold intervals, it is best that you perform them on your road bike. As I have mentioned before, riding and training on your road bike is less stressful on your body and therefore you can recover more quickly from the training ride. You can then perform more intense training with less rest time. By doing intervals on the road or trainer, you can monitor the intensity more easily as well as keep the intensity more consistent. For example, if I were scheduled to do an interval session of 3×20 minutes with a 15-minute easy spin in between each interval I would either find a hill or rolling road section that would allow me to sustain a high heart rate with out any long stops or downhill sections. When you are on the mountain bike on trails, it is difficult to find a trail that would force you to keep a constant heart rate or wattage unless you find a long hill. Trails are usually more rolling or they have obstacles that may force you to go harder or get off your bike.

There is, however, a good time to do lactate threshold intervals and PC jumps on your mountain bike, and that is when it gets closer to the race season. Once you have a good base of fitness and need to work on more specific skills for mountain biking, it is time to get on the trails. At this point doing LT intervals and PC jumps on the trails is a great idea and important for getting you tuned up to race. Doing these intervals on the trails will force you to keep your intensity up even on a flat or rolling section. It will also give you a chance to work on sprinting on the dirt. Living in Colorado, we don't necessarily have a choice in when we ride on the trails; the snow and mud levels determine it. If you are more fortunate and can ride on trails all year long, you may want to wait to do intervals on the trails until 6 to 8 weeks before your first race.

SPECIALIZATION PHASE II

Now that your body has learned how to tolerate and clear lactic acid and you are a sprinting machine, it is time to start in to the specialization II phase. The second part of the specialization phase involves fine-tuning your maximum effort intervals also called $\dot{V}O_2$ max intervals. Because it is getting close to race season, it is also important to work on your technical skills and any weaknesses that you may have. This is also a good time to jump in to some training races as well as practicing your starts. Doing a few practice races in your area is also a good idea. This will give you some feedback on how your training is going and most likely push you to train harder.

$\dot{V}O_2$ Capacity

$\dot{V}O_2$max is the maximum amount of oxygen that your body can deliver to your muscles within a certain period of time. Your body can sustain this level of oxygen consumption only for a short time and only when you put forth maximum effort. Your $\dot{V}O_2$max is generally determined by your genetic makeup, but it can be increased by up to 10 percent with training.

The only true way of determining your $\dot{V}O_2$max is by getting tested in a physiology lab. This will tell you what your heart rate, or watts, should be when you're doing $\dot{V}O_2$ intervals. If you don't have access to a lab but you have tested yourself for your maximal heart rate, when you do these intervals you should be at zone 5, or between 90 to 100 percent of your maximum. Look at the chart in chapter 9 for more information.

Because $\dot{V}O_2$max levels can be sustained only for a short period, anywhere from 1 to 8 minutes, your intervals should be only that long. As with all intervals, you need a good 15- to 20-minute warm-up before doing an interval session. It is also a good idea to do two or three 30-second to 1-minute sprints on the bike after having done your warm-up but before doing full intervals because this will get your body ready for a hard, sustained effort. This is just a tip to help with the $\dot{V}O_2$ intervals; it is not mandatory to perform them. Even if you do the sprints, you can be sure that the first one or two $\dot{V}O_2$max intervals you do will be difficult. I have found, however, that once you get your heart rate to the appropriate level, it is easier to sustain. Just trying to get the heart rate up is difficult.

$\dot{V}O_2$max intervals can last from 2 to 8 minutes. Generally the rest time in between intervals is just as long as the intervals themselves. So if you are doing a 3-minute interval, you should spin easily for 3 minutes before going on to the next interval. As with every interval or workout I have discussed thus far, you should slowly work up so that you don't overstress your body and injure yourself. The way to do this is to start off with 2- to 3-minute intervals and work up in time and repetitions (see table 10.2).

Table 10.2   4-Week Build for $\dot{V}O_2$max Intervals

Week 1	Two days of three $\dot{V}O_2$max interval sessions of 3 minutes each, with a 3-minute easy spin in between each
Week 2	Two days of four $\dot{V}O_2$max interval sessions of 3 minutes each, with a 3-minute easy spin in between each
Week 3	Two days of five $\dot{V}O_2$max interval sessions of 3 minutes each, with a 3-minute easy spin in between each
Week 4	(easy week) Two days of two $\dot{V}O_2$max interval sessions of 3 minutes each, with a 3-minute easy spin in between each

To make these sessions less monotonous, you can change the times of the intervals in one session. For example, one day of intervals could be 2, 3, 4, 3, and 2 minutes long with a 4-minute easy spin in between each. You can also make the interval sessions similar to a race situation. In a race there is not a prescribed amount of time that you will be at $\dot{V}O_2max$, or a specific amount of time in between these efforts, so changing the times around can be beneficial.

Strengths and Weaknesses

In the specialization II phase of training, you should work on your strengths and weaknesses to get you ready for races. You must first determine what your strengths and weaknesses are. This should not be difficult if you are honest with yourself and your coach. This is one of the first things I ask an athlete when I begin working with him: "What do you feel you are good at and what could you improve on?" If he has a tough time determining his strengths and weaknesses, this is what I list: climbing, descending, rocky terrain, wet roots, rolling hills, long flat sections, starts, and cornering. I am sure you can think of more areas of concern, but this list should get you thinking. You should already be addressing some of these weaknesses in your training sessions. For example, if you don't feel strong at the end of a race, the endurance portion of the training will help you. If you tend to slow down on flat sections, which is something I had always done, make sure you do the LT and $\dot{V}O_2$ intervals on flat sections as well as on climbs.

You can address many of your technical weaknesses by going out to practice on the trails. During this time of the training season, I have an athlete do one fun ride a week on the mountain bike, or I will call it a technical workout session. This should get the athlete used to riding the mountain bike again and will give her a chance to hone skills without pressure to perform specific intervals. If I know the rider has certain weaknesses, such as riding wet roots, I will suggest a trail that will force her to work on that skill. There may not always be a trail in your area that will simulate the skills you are looking to improve on, but do the best you can.

Don't neglect your strengths. Although you need to improve your weaknesses, it is also important to hone your strengths. If you like to climb, make sure that when out for that fun technical ride, do some hard climbs in between working on the descending. Or if you like to descend but have a problem with cornering, pick a fun descent that has a few tight switchbacks and do that portion of the trail a few times before the fun section. Getting good at technical skills takes a lot of time and practice, but fun is the name of the game. If you are trying to do a section of the trail and are getting frustrated, move on.

Starts

Whether you're good at starts or not, now is the time to practice, because race season is just around the corner. It only makes sense to work on skills that you will be using in the race, closest to race season. This allows your mind and body to get prepared. As with building a house, you first work on the blueprint, you then work on the structure, and then you do the finishing work or fine detail.

The best way to practice your starts is by making them as similar to a true race start as possible. Although you should try to do this for all aspects of your training, this is most true when working on starts. I like to get a group of four or five riders together on the trail. I designate a starting line and have everyone line up as they would on a true start line. Because we will be doing this several times, everyone should get a chance to line up in different positions. For example, if you are in the front the first few times, try lining up behind someone the third or fourth time. Throw in different sections of trail as well. Practice on an open stretch that funnels into a left-hand turn or a steep climb. Again, make it as true to a rear start as possible.

I generally have the starts be a 15-second sprint and then a 5-minute easy spin before going again. I have also used a 15-second sprint start followed by a 5-minute LT interval before taking a 5-minute easy spin. The harder and more racelike you make any interval, the easier it will be during an actual race. If you are not so fortunate to scare up a group of willing starters, you can practice on your own. As you are riding, either on your mountain or road bike, come to a complete stop and clip out of your pedal. Visualize the start and "on your mark, get set, go," sprint as hard as you can for 15 seconds.

These intervals not only will help you to become more physically efficient at starting, but you will also learn some techniques. For example, what gear should you be in? What side is smoother for clipping in? Where to line up if the first turn is to the left? Practice makes perfect. Whoever said that must have been a racer.

Training Races

Part of your specialization II phase of training should involve some training races. I can tell you from experience that it is crucial to do some practice races before doing a more important race. This can be anything from an evening pickup race series to a road race in your area. What you will find, most likely, is that you have not been training as hard as you should have. Every season of my race career, I would do one of the early-season races either in Moab, Utah, or in California. And in every one of those races I did worse than I had expected. For one, it takes me several races to warm up. Two, I thought I was training hard enough but I obviously was not. There was only one time where I kicked butt on my first race and that was after doing two 2.5-hour rides on my indoor trainer with six 7- to 8-minute $\dot{V}O_2$ intervals. That was also the first race in 2000 that I had to win in order to get on the long team for the Olympics.

COMPETITION PHASE

Now that you have done your training, it is time to race, which means you have reached the competition phase. The competition phase is built around staying fresh for races as well as fine tuning your skills. It is also the time where you need to taper your training which will help your body recover and be strong for race day.

Because competition phase can be difficult when setting up ones training schedule, I would like to give you an idea of what it entails. In a perfect world, the racer will have at least 4 weeks in between their "peak" races. If this is the case, I will have the athlete slowly ramp up in both time and intensity over the next two weeks, with the first week being more for recovery. The third week will be a taper or easy week, and the fourth week or the week of the race will again have a slight increase in time and intensity.

If the athlete has more than 4 weeks in between each peak, you can use the same format but have them ramp up in time and intensity more gradually. If they have a shorter span of time in between each peak, the athlete will get a shorter ramp-up phase. Whatever you do, don't neglect the rest in between. If an athlete has followed a fairly regimented training schedule leading up to their first peak race, they will most likely keep a good level of fitness during the competition phase. The key during this phase is to keep them from overtraining or getting sick.

Table 10.3 on page 164 is an example of rider A's schedule, as discussed in chapter 8. She will have a total of 5 weeks in between two of her peak races: On July 30 she is peaking for a World Cup and on September 4 she is peaking for the World Championships.

Tapering

Now that you have done all of your training, worked on specific skills, and done a few training races, it is time to taper for your first peak race. Tapering means to decrease the amount of time or intensity of your workouts. In training, this is done on a smaller scale every fourth or sixth week, depending on the length of your training block. Tapering, most notably, is done before every important, or peak, race. This is one of the reasons, when setting up a schedule, that an athlete or coach needs to work back from the first peak race to work the taper in correctly.

TYPICAL TRAINING WEEK

Neal Henderson

© Courtesy of Scott Schumacher

"During the competition phase if you are racing two or more weeks in a row this is an example of what my typical week might look like:

Sunday--Race Monday— Easy recovery spin: 30-60 minutes, high cadence, HR zone 1/recovery.

Tuesday--If tired, off. Otherwise, 1-1.5-hour endurance ride, HR zone 2-3 (sub-lactate threshold), with optional short bursts with full recovery between.

Wednesday—Short-track, cross-country race or simulated race effort. Include a mix of intensities from HR zone 3-5 or endurance through $\dot{V}O_2$ max. Try to limit $\dot{V}O_2$ max effort to 3-8 minutes, and lactate threshold effort to 10-20 minutes. Short (1-2 minute) intervals could also be substituted.

Thursday--Recovery spin, 30-60 minutes, HR zone 1.

Friday--Off/travel. Or relax and stretch for mental training!

Saturday--Prerace ride. Preview the course if possible. Ride 1-2 hours with several 1-3 minute long race-paced efforts, with full recovery between. Take time on technical sections to learn the best line, and know when and where to mount and dismount. Do this ride early in the day, and then get off your feet away from the race and relax.

Sunday--Race. Be sure to warm-up well, doing 20-30 minutes of progressive riding in HR zones 1-3 riding. Then include 3 bouts of 2-minute $\dot{V}O_2$ intervals with full recovery between. Finish warm-up in time to get to the start line in good position. Stay relaxed until the start, and then execute the race, paying attention to details!

When and how long an athlete tapers depend on the athlete. Some athletes feel best if they taper during the week of the race. Other athletes feel best if they taper during the week before the race. I suggest you try both methods to find out what works best for you.

One other form of tapering is also done in the days leading up to a peak race. Whether you are taking that week easy or using it as a build week, what you choose to do on those days just before your peak race will involve some form of tapering. In this section, I educate you on when to taper, why you need to taper, and how you should taper.

The main reason for tapering at any stage is to give your body a rest. When you take an easy week by lightening the intensity or hours on the bike, you give your body a chance to rest and rebuild those muscles that have been stressed. When you are training hard, you are basically taking your body to the limit. With this, you are overstressing the cardio-respiratory system as well as tearing muscle fibers. To get a benefit from this workload, you need to have a period of easy workouts with some rest days in between. After this rest period you should then be stronger because your body has had a chance to adapt to the stresses put on it. Your body is then able to push harder, go faster, and tolerate more stress.

Not only does the taper week give you a physical rest, but it also gives you a mental rest from the time and intensity of being on the bike. When you are constantly on the bike, you are susceptible to both mental and physical burnout. It is important to take yourself right up to the edge of burnout with out pushing yourself over. This is called overreaching versus overtraining.

There are three different times to taper. One is after a block of training, which may be every fourth, sixth, or eighth week. My athletes and I taper every fourth week. It may change throughout the season or throughout a career, but it is a good idea to follow a plan and stick with it as closely as possible.

True tapering takes effect the week or two weeks before your peak race. I think that tapering two weeks before a race is the most effective, but you have to find what works for you. What I have found is that when taking the week of the race easy, I will be "flat" or "stale" and have no strength or speed during the race. If you take it easy the week before the race, you will then have time to adapt to your training and be able to reacquaint your body with some high-intensity efforts. This will remind your body what it needs to do, both physically and mentally, during the race. For example, if you are doing an ultra-distance race, you may choose to have several weeks of tapering before the race. You can play around with this, especially with those easy-season races or races that are not as important. Don't worry—experimenting won't cause you to have a bad race; it will just help you fine-tune what works best for you.

Table 10.3 6-Week Training Cycle

Wk #	Date	Mon July 25	Tues July 26	Wed July 27	Thurs July 28	Fri July 29	Sat July 30	Sun July 31	h/wk
1 Competition phase	**Planned workout**	Easy spin/Off	Power starts in a 2.0-h ride	$\dot{V}O_2$ intervals in a 2.5-h ride	Easy spin/Off; Travel day	Prerace day warm-up of 1.5 h on the course	Race for 3 h	Fun, easy ride for 1 h	10
	Actual workout								
									0:00
									0:00

	Date	Aug 1	Aug 2	Aug 3	Aug 4	Aug 5	Aug 6	Aug 7	
2 Competition phase— Recovery week	**Planned workout**	Easy spin/Off	Easy spin of 1 h	Sprint intervals in a 1.0-h ride	Hill repeats, in a 1.5-h ride	Easy spin/Off	Hill repeats in a 2.0-h ride	Fun ride of whatever you would like for 1-1.5 h	6-7
	Actual workout								
									0:00
									0:00

	Date	Aug 8	Aug 9	Aug 10	Aug 11	Aug 12	Aug 13	Aug 14	
3 Competition phase— Spec I/II rebuild	**Planned workout**	Easy spin/Off	Sprint intervals or 6 × 15 sec in a 2.0-h ride	Hill repeats of 3 × 10 min in a 2.0-h ride	Easy spin/Off	Strength/ Endurance intervals of 4 × 5 min in a 1.5-h ride	Hill Repeats of 4 × 10 min in a 2.5-h ride	Fun mountain bike ride working on technical skills in 3.0 h	11
	Actual workout								
									0:00
									0:00

Table 10.3 (continued)

		Mon	Tues	Wed	Thurs	Fri	Sat	Sun	
	Date	**Aug 15**	**Aug 16**	**Aug 17**	**Aug 18**	**Aug 19**	**Aug 20**	**Aug 21**	
4 Competition phase— Spec I/II rebuild	**Planned workout**	Easy spin/ Off	Sprint intervals of 7 × 1 min in a 2.0-h ride	Hill repeats of 3 × 15 min in a 2.5-h ride	Easy spin/Off	Prerace day warm-up in a 1.5-h ride	Local race for 3.0 h	Fun mountain bike ride working on technical skills for 3.0 h	12
	Actual workout								
									0:00
									0:00

	Date	**Aug 22**	**Aug 23**	**Aug 24**	**Aug 25**	**Aug 26**	**Aug 27**	**Aug 28**	
5 Competition phase— Taper	**Planned workout**	Easy spin/ Off	Sprints of 4 × 15 sec in a 1.0-h ride	Hill repeats of 2 × 10 min in a 1.5-h ride	Easy spin/Off	Strength/ Endurance intervals of 3 × 5 min in a 1.5-h ride	$\dot{V}O_2$ intervals of 4 × 4 min in a 2.0-h ride	Fun mountain bike ride working on technical skills in a 2.0-h ride	8
	Actual Workout								
									0:00
									0:00

	Date	**Aug 29**	**Aug 30**	**Aug 31**	**Sept 1**	**Sept 2**	**Sept 3**	**Sept 4**	
6 Competition phase— Race	**Planned workout**	Easy spin/ Off Travel to the race	Sprints of 5 × 15 sec in a 1.5-h ride	Hill repeats of 3 × 10 min in a 2.0-hour ride	Preride the course for 2.0 h working on technical skills	Easy spin/ Off	Prerace day warm-up on the course for 1.5 h	Race World Champion-ships	10
	Actual workout								

The week of an important race can also be thought of as a form of tapering. Again, you can choose to take an easy day the day before a race, two days before the race, or even three days before the race. When I first started racing, I would do an easy spin the day before the race and stay away from the venue. What I found was that I started to get nervous on that day anyway, so it wasn't very restful. I then changed to taking an easy day two days before my race and doing some hard efforts the day before the race. This ensured that I would get some true relaxation on the easy day and then wake my body up again and get it ready the day before the race. Figure it out and then stick with it. Once you find what works for you, you can make it a part of your routine.

OVERREACHING VERSUS OVERTRAINING

Most athletes have heard the word *overtraining,* which generally has negative connotations. Overreaching, on the other hand, is a fairly new term for a concept that has been around for a while.

Overreaching is the point in an athlete's training plan that involves pushing the body as hard as it can tolerate and then resting. If all goes well, this should happen every third week of a four-week training block. Then once the athlete has had a rest week, the body is able to adapt and become even stronger in order to tolerate the next three-week session.

Overtraining is what occurs when an athlete is pushed too hard during training. The body is then unable to recover with a rest week; in fact, it needs several weeks or months of little to no riding before recovery is possible. In other words, the season is shot. Some coaches feel that taking an athlete to the overtraining state for one season will give the athlete an idea of how much he can tolerate. Therefore, in future seasons the athlete and coach will know just how much time and intensity the athlete can handle. I don't subscribe to this method because I think the negative effects far outweigh the positive effects. Unless the athlete is in the teens or early 20s, it is difficult to give up a season of racing. This can lead to giving up on the sport altogether. Also, I am not sold on the fact that one can then determine exactly what the athlete can and cannot tolerate because several things can lead to overtraining.

Acute exercise stimulus leads to acute fatigue that in turn leads to overreaching. However you have to be very careful not to cross the line from overreaching into overtraining. Overreaching is a positive adaptation if used correctly but overtraining is maladaptation of the stimulus and therefore leads to decreased performance.

How will you know whether you are getting to that overtraining stage? Keep a training log and watch for the signs and symptoms. The following are some of the basic things to watch for:

1. Consistent decrease in performance compared to early in the season or the previous season
2. Need for prolonged recovery after workouts and competition
3. Reduction in ability to tolerate training
4. Increased heart rate at rest, during exercise, and during recovery
5. Decrease in total body weight
6. Poor sleep quality and chronic fatigue
7. Loss of appetite and stomach pain
8. Muscle soreness and increased injury
9. Increased susceptibility to colds, flu, and allergies
10. Bacterial infection and slow healing of minor cuts
11. General apathy and lethargy
12. Mood changes

These are just a few things to watch for when undertaking a training program. You need to show more than one of these signs before determining you are at the overtraining stage. After having trained for several years, you will have a good idea when you are getting to that stage. I know when I am getting to the overtraining stage because I am overtired and have difficulty recovering even after resting. I have difficulty sleeping at night, which is not normal for me. I also tend to get a sore throat, which turns into a full-blown illness if I don't take it easy. Take notice of your body and watch what it is telling you, or write it down in your training journal. You can then go back and see if you increased the intensity or duration too rapidly or if you were unable to get enough rest.

Among the things I have my athletes write down in their training logs are resting heart rate, quality of sleep, how they feel that day, how their training went, appetite, mood, and maybe weight. Most people don't take time to write in their logs. I was actually one of those people, and most of the athletes I train don't do a good job of it. What I ask is for them to monitor these things for a month in the early season so we can establish a baseline. Then, if they think they may be overtraining, I have them take note of those same factors to see if there is a change. After several years of training, you will learn to see the signs before they become a problem, but until then you should get a journal and take notes.

If you think you may be getting to the overtraining stage, take a week of easy training or take a week completely off training. Once you have taken a week off, reevaluate yourself for the signs and symptoms of over-training. If you continue to show signs of overtraining, take another week of either easy training or complete rest from training. Once you begin to have signs of overtraining, it is a good idea to make an appointment with a doctor. A general checkup and blood test can help to determine whether you are low on such nutrients as iron, which may contribute to the symptoms of overtraining. Once you are feeling better, slowly ramp up your training; don't go right back at the level where you left off. For example, you are supposed to be in specification phase I and you are in your third week performing three 15-minute LT intervals in a 15-hour week. If you have taken one to two weeks off and are feeling much better, you would then start back at your easy week of that phase and ramp up again. It isn't worth taking a chance on trashing your whole season if you are feeling sick or have signs of overtraining. I know many people don't listen to their bodies and just pile on the training even if they are feeling weak or tired; they simply have a hard time taking it easy. The saying "more is better" doesn't always apply. It's very important to back off on your training if you are not feeling well. If you don't, you will pay the consequences later on.

There are many causes of overtraining. The most obvious is that you have physically done too much. Several other reasons, which you may not always take into account, are relationship problems, problems with family or friends, financial problems, and feelings of insecurity about a job. All of these things will put increased stress on your body; if you then add some intense training, down you go. I worked with sport psychologist Othon Kesend for several years before I made the Olympic team. One of the ways in which he helped me was to clarify how much I could and could not tolerate regarding both training and the psychosocial aspects of my life. He helped me to deal with those things that I could not change and make adjustments or cut out what I didn't need to do. For instance, I needed to work in order to live. Othon and I discussed exactly how much I needed to work and what job would be best for me to have while I continued training. Many people may think that a sport psychologist is a frill, but it may be what you need to get you to your goals, and they are well worth the money.

ELEVEN

Planning Before the Race

© Courtesy of Rob Karman

Now that you have your goals and races set and have done your training and worked on your skills, you are ready to race! You may think that what you have done so far will make you a stellar racer. But guess what—you have more to learn. In this chapter I educate you on the fine points of preracing. This includes what you need to do when traveling and what is out of your control and therefore what you should not worry about. You will know what to look for when riding a course and how to make up your own race-day routine.

TRAVEL AND LODGING

To decrease the stress around race time, make sure your travel and lodging are in order before you leave for the race. Don't wait until the last minute. Most race information packets will give you some ideas of where to stay and phone numbers to call for the host hotel. Give the host hotel a call and ask for numbers to other hotels or possible lodging in the area. Another good source is the tourist information center in that town or region. Seasoned racers are also a good resource on where to stay. I don't care how you do it, but figure out where you will be staying before you get to the race.

Once you know where you will be staying, arrange how you will get to and from your lodging. If you will be flying to the town where you will race, make sure you have a rental car or find a shuttle that will take you to the hotel. If you are taking the shuttle or a train, make sure they run late at night, because you don't know if your flight will be delayed.

A great way to travel is with other cyclists. That way you can share the expenses (we know most of us racers are broke). Strike up a conversation with people at some of the local races and pick their brains about who may be going to other races. Join a local team so that you can share lodging and travel expenses. You can even call or e-mail the race promoter to see if they have any ideas about people who would be willing to share travel arrangements or lodging. For the most part, mountain bike racers are very friendly and willing to help each other out. Don't be afraid to ask.

The final tip about travel is to have a plan B and maybe even a plan C. You can bet that something will delay you or mess up some part of your travel plans, so make sure you have a way of contacting whomever you plan to stay with or travel with. For example, if someone is planning to pick you up from the airport, have a plan for contacting that person if your flight is delayed or cancelled. This can be either a call to a cell phone or a message left at the hotel or house where you will be staying or even at your home, where you can check the messages.

As a worst-case scenario, you should talk with any other racers that may be on your flight and ask them how they are getting to the venue. I have been known to hitch a ride from people who were picking up bike cases at the oversized baggage claim. However, unless you don't care when and if you will be making it to the race, I would suggest you get your lodging and travel to and from the race as secure as possible in advance.

PACKING YOUR GEAR

As you begin to think of what to pack, start with a list of necessary equipment and clothing and consider the availability of food and the type of climate your traveling into. It's essential that you come well-prepared for any eventuality if you want to do your absolute best.

Making a List

Generate a list of what you need to pack. For some of us, the packing and traveling can be very stressful. I have composed a list of items to remember. This is not exhaustive, because everyone has specific needs, but it is a good place to start:

Bike

Helmet

Shoes

Glasses

Clothes: 2 or 3 pair of shorts, 2 or 3 jerseys, 2 or 3 pair of socks, gloves, knee or leg warmers, arm warmers, rain jacket, vest

Equipment: Tubes, tires, multitool, tire pump, CO_2 cartridge (you may need to buy this at your destination because most airlines don't let you travel with one), pump for shocks, tire iron, chain tool, mudguard

Cleaning equipment: Simple Green or degreaser, sponge, bucket (if you can fit it in your bike bag when flying), brush, rag, chain lube

Party clothes

Pillow

Ear plugs and eye mask

Drink mix, energy bars, and gel

If you're traveling by plane, all of the items that you packed in your bike bag or box may be in limbo. You may be greeted by your bike bag at your destination, but your clothes bag may be in another country. One way to avoid this is to check the flight tag when the ticket person attaches it to your bag. The tag should list where your bags will be going and the final destination. The next best thing to do is to take anything in your carry-on bag that you cannot easily replace or do without. Well, you can't take your bike, but I would suggest you take your shoes and your pedals. You may be able to borrow a bike and some bike clothes from someone else at the race. You can bet you won't find anyone who is willing to lend you shoes. Your helmet is another item that you might consider as carry-on baggage. Helmets are not too difficult to fit on board, but the likelihood of buying one or borrowing one is not very good.

I will never forget traveling to Switzerland for a world championship race only to find out my bike hadn't come with me. I arrived in Switzerland in the morning after having traveled solo for several hours, and my bike did not show up at the baggage claim. At that point I made my way to the baggage counter to ask where I could find oversized bags, and they informed me that my bike did not make it on the same flight, Horrors! The nice airline people gave me a bag full of the usual toiletries and had me fill out a description of my bag. This was the point at which I began crying and telling them that this was my bike and I needed it for a world championship race and blubber, blubber, boo, hoo! The person behind the counter, a Swiss person who spoke great English, acted very calm and told me she would get my bike to the venue. Well, guess what? It took me three train transfers and about three hours to get up to Châteaudeau, Switzerland, and I couldn't imagine that my bike would ever get there.

I got to Châteaudeau late that afternoon, got my room, met the other racers I would be staying with, and promptly went to sleep. First thing the next morning, I called the airline, and they told me to call back in the afternoon. I called back that afternoon and they said my bike would arrive the next morning. I spent the rest of the day trying to stay calm and walking part of the racecourse. I then hiked up to the train station that next morning and looked at the schedule. My bike hadn't made the first train, so I planned to hike back up around noon. I called the airline again and they assured me my bike was on its way. I talked with some of the other racers about the possibility of borrowing a bike and then proceeded to walk back to the train station. "Oh my, I think that is my bike bag!" I felt as though I had been reunited with my mother after years of forced separation. I couldn't believe my bike had made it! The moral of the story is that if it is out of your control, there is nothing you can do about it but stay calm. Things will work themselves out.

Braving the Elements

Another key part of traveling for mountain bikers, especially in foreign countries, are food and weather. Food is obviously very important for a smooth-running body. You should know what your body runs well on and what makes you happy. Often, if you are traveling to a foreign country or just to another state, the food you are accustomed to may not be available and therefore the food itself becomes an adventure! If that is the case, you should bring some food with you. (See chapter 12 for specific examples on nutrition.)

One of the world championship races was at a ski resort in Spain. I knew beforehand that they would have to ship food up the mountain for us and therefore the quality of food would be questionable. I decided to bring my own cereal, dried fruit, nuts, and canned tuna to make sure I would have some of the food I liked to eat. After hanging out with Ruthie Matthes, I also discovered the need for a hot pot and an outlet adaptor. A hot pot is basically an electric teapot that allows you to heat up water for tea or even cook soup, oatmeal, and hard-boiled eggs. You could have a regular picnic in the privacy of your hotel room. Don't get too picky, though. If you are stressing about food, you are wasting energy that you need to use during your race.

And then there's the weather. If you don't know the type of climate of the region you will be visiting, find out. With the widespread availability of the Internet, it's easy to find out what the typical weather is for any time of year in any area of the world. Once you find out, pack the appropriate clothing. Or, always pack for the worst possible scenario

© Icon Sports Media

Riders brave the elements from mountains to mudslides during the Mountain Bike World Cup in Ft. William, Scotland.

and never forget your mudguard. It is better to be overprepared than underprepared.

I think one reason mountain bike racing is so fun is that you never know what to expect. Weather is always a mystery. In 1999, we had a World Cup race in Canmore, Canada. We had raced there the year before so had some idea of what to expect. The weather was fairly cool and there was a good chance of rain. I remember in the previous year, we were all scrambling to make mud flaps out of plastic milk cartons because we hadn't expected rain. Well, we were prepared for the rain this time, and it came. What we didn't expect was the cold weather. When we started the race, the temperature was in the 40s and it was gray and cloudy. It is always hard to know what to wear during the warm-up and during the race, because you tend to get hot. After the warm-up and when sitting on the start line we all started stripping down. It was pretty cold out but we didn't want to overheat either. "On your mark, get set, go!" And off we went into the back woods of the Canmore ski resort. The first two laps were no problem. It was cold and drizzling, but I didn't notice because I was concentrating on picking people off because I started in the back of the pack. "Okay, what are those white flakes? Is that my head getting dizzy or is it snowing? It is snowing!" Being the hard-core racer that I was, I just started to laugh. So we did at least two laps of the 6-mile loop in the snow. At one point I couldn't shift or brake because my fingers were too numb. I had to slow down and shake my arms around to get some blood flow. I can't remember where I finished but the true feat was just to finish. I do remember trying to talk with John and Andy, who were helping us after the race, and I couldn't even get the words out because my lips were numb. The truly awesome part was the spectators. Those Canadians are a hardy bunch. They were still all over the course yelling for us even though it was cold and snowing. If they weren't there, I think I may have ridden off into oblivion, not knowing what I was doing. I also heard afterwards that one of the spectators gave Sheri Cain a jacket to wear during the race. If you have raced at all, I am sure you have your own weather stories to tell. Learn from them! Bring clothes for all types of weather and don't be afraid to wear them.

PRERIDING THE RACECOURSE

If at all possible, you should ride the course at least once before you race on it. This does no mean getting on it and riding the hour before the race, unless the course is only a 15- to 20- minute loop. This means either the day before or several days before the race, plan to get on the course and check it out. The reason to preride the course is to familiarize yourself with as much of it as possible. Some of the most important things to look at while preriding are the start line, the finish line, and the technical sections and whether you should ride or run them. It's also a good idea to know where the feed zones are, where double tracks funnel, and how to deal with changing conditions.

- Starting lines. Even if you are not able to preride the whole course, take a look at the start line. Look for the best line to start on. Usually the course starts on a dirt road because you want the racers to be spread out. On most dirt roads there are tire tracks. The tire tracks will be the place where the dirt is more packed down, and around the tracks the dirt will be loose. The best place to line up is where the dirt is more packed down so that you don't slide out or the person in front of you doesn't slide out. If you are lucky enough to line up in the front, you should be as close to the hard-packed surface as possible.

The other aspect of the start line I look for is which way the first turn in the course goes. For example, the course may start off straight, but 500 yards into it, it turns to the left. In this situation, you should be on the right side. If you are in the front line or several rows back, it would be a good idea for you to be on the right side when lining up. When everyone hits that first left-hand turn, they will all wedge in to the left and create a bottleneck on that side while those people on the right will have a more open path to ride around.

- Finish lines. The next thing you should look at on the course is the finish line. The finish line may be the same as the start line, which would make it easy to check out if you don't have the luxury of looking at the whole course. You'll want to see what the finish line looks like in case the race comes down to a sprint finish, so keep this in mind when practicing. A sprint finish does not often happen in a mountain bike race, but it definitely can, and you want to be prepared for anything.

At the finish line, look for characteristics similar to those at the start line. For instance, where is the smoothest line leading up to the finish, where is the last corner, and how far from that corner is the finish line? To get a good idea of the best line leading up to the finish, backtrack from the finish line at least 25 yards.

First I like to look for the best line, which means the smoothest and hardest-packed surface. Sometimes this can be out on the sides where there is grass. Next I look at how far away the last corner is from the finish line and where I should be going into that corner. If the last corner is 25 feet away from the finish, during a sprint make sure you are the first one out of that corner, because that is who will win the race. This may mean taking the inside line, because the person on the outside will have a longer distance to travel. Remember, the shortest distance between two points is a line, not a curve. This technique may seem a little cutthroat, but hey, as long as you don't take the other person out, the first person to the finish line wins.

- Technical sections. One of the primary reasons to look at a race-course before the race is to make sure you have no surprises. The main surprise would be in the form of a brutal technical section. If you had no clue where the section was located on the course, you may slow your pace throughout the first lap in order to be prepared or you may come flying into it and take a huge digger.

When practicing the technical sections, first you'll want to determine whether it is rideable for you. Notice I mentioned *for you*. There have been several gnarly technical sections that I have decided not to ride, knowing other fellow racers were clearing. For example, Bailey's Bailout on the Vail, Colorado, course was a 5-foot—no lie—rocky drop-off that landed a rider on a rocky single-track trail. I had no qualms about dismounting and jumping down from that rock with my bike on my shoulder even knowing full well that Sarah Ballantyne and Julie Furtado were riding it. I was not prepared to die for that race.

As I have talked about in the chapters on technical skills, you have several things to look at when practicing a technical section. First off, can

By preriding the race course you'll feel comfortable and prepared as you approach the starting line.

PRERACE REGIMEN

Heather Szabo

© Courtesy of Rob Karman

"My main focus on a race morning is fuel—breakfast is very important! If the race is an early start, I try to finish eating about three hours before the start of the race. If the race is early afternoon, I try to eat early, then I eat another small meal about three hours before the start. I've found the race breakfast that works for me is two eggs (cooked over-medium) and a plain bagel with all-natural peanut butter.

About two hours before the start of the race, I make sure everything is ready to go—chain lubed, tire pressure, water bottles. If it is a multiple-lap race and I'm getting feeds I make sure the bottles are labeled with my name and what lap I want them.

About 90 minutes before the start, I chamois up! This is a good time to top off food stores by nibbling a Clif Bar. I also start warming up on the bike. I've found a good long warm-up works well for me—about 20 minutes of continuous, easy riding followed by several short (1-3 minutes) hard, high-intensity efforts. If the race starts with a long climb, I'll do one longer sustained climb, maybe even on the course if it is possible. After that, it's just several trips to the bathroom (race nerves do wonders for the bladder!) and visualizing the start of the race."

you ride it without crashing, or should you run? Second, what is the fastest line? When most of us come up on a questionable technical section, we will stand at the top and watch others go down. That can be a good idea, but if you don't ride it after 5 minutes of watching, run it. You can always try it again on the next loop. If you aren't able to ride the section at least 70 percent of the time without crashing, run it.

There can be more than one line through a technical section. The best way to go is obviously the fastest line. However, if the fast line is more difficult to ride, go for the safer line. The way to determine what line is the quickest is either to time yourself on both or to practice them with a fellow racer. Both of you come into the section at the same time and, taking a different route through, see who makes it to the end first.

• Running sections. As I have discussed in chapter 6, running isn't always a bad idea. If you have decided to run a section, either because it is too dangerous to ride or it is faster to run, you should be sure to practice. Truly the hard part is determining whether you will run or not. Once you have made that decision, the running part isn't that difficult. The reason to practice is to have fewer things to worry about during the race. You want to determine where you will dismount and remount your bike as well as what path you will take to run.

Pretend you are in a race situation and come up to the section as fast as possible and dismount. Then find the quickest way to run the sections and remount. You may have to run a little farther than you would like in order to find a good section in which to remount your bike, but make sure you can smoothly pedal out instead of getting back on too soon. The one example that comes to mind is a rocky technical section, with a wooden bridge, on the Vermont National course. Once I got over the bridge, the trail continued to be a single-track rocky climb. It was easy to get back on the bike after going over the bridge, but without enough speed and momentum, I was unable to make it over the rocks on the climb out. It was better to continue running a little farther to where the trail became less technical in order to remount, but you can bet there was no lack of trying.

- Feed zones. When preriding a course, always look for the feed zones. The feed zone is the designated area on the course where the racer can be handed a bottle or food. Depending on the size of the loop, there will be either one or two feed zones. First determine which one is the easiest from which to grab a bottle. Second, can you take a drink after receiving your bottle, or do you need to put it in your bottle cage and wait for a smoother section of the course? Third, before you reach the feed zone, make sure to drink all of the liquid in the bottle you already have. It is a good motivating factor to get you to drink up.

After I have done a lap to look at the technical sections, on the next lap I find where I can eat and drink. By eating, I mean consume a gel, not have a picnic. The obvious places to look for are flat double-track sections or maybe a gradual open climb. When you get to these sections, get your water bottle out and take a swig for practice. Of course you will be going faster and may be a bit out of breath during the race, but know that when you are on these sections of the course, you need to drink. Again, this will take the guesswork out during the race so that you can put your energy into hammering.

- Double track funneling into single track. Know where the double track funnels into a single track. The most crucial part in the course at which to be aware of the funneling effect is at the beginning. Generally the first time you get to the single track after the start, there will be a huge bottleneck. The best place to be in a bottleneck is in the front. If you are in the middle or back, you can wave good-bye to the top 10 racers. This is another reason why you want to practice your starts. If you can hurt for the first 5 to 10 minutes of the race, just enough to be one of the top 10 to the first single track, half the battle is over. Now all you have to do is hold your position.

It is also a good idea to take note of some of the other sections that funnel into single track, especially if it turns into a climb or technical downhill. In these cases, you want to make sure you are either in front or at least not behind someone who you know is slower than you. I don't care if you have to sprint out of the saddle to get there; make sure you are in a good position. Otherwise you will be losing precious time. You can always rest when the race is over.

- Changing conditions. The last thing you need to remember when looking at the course is that it can change! If you are able to check out the course the afternoon before race day, it will most likely not change too much. The course will also not change too much if the conditions are dry and hard packed. If, however, the conditions are wet and the rain continues, you can bet the course will change every lap. In this case get the general layout and don't stress. All of the other racers will have the same disadvantage.

One of the most important things I was taught by Othon Kesend, my sport psychologist, was not to spend time stressing about things that were out of my control, such as delayed flights, missing baggage, and the weather. Do the best you can to plan ahead. Bring gear for all types of weather as well as food in case you run into delays in your travels or have difficulty getting to a store at your destination. Lastly, if at all possible, preride the course. Knowing what you are up against in the form of corners after the start line, gnarly drop-offs, and bottlenecks into single-track sections will help take away some of the guesswork. Now get out there and race!

TWELVE

Riding to Win

Getting into a routine of what to do the day of your race is key to decreasing stress. The less energy you expend on being stressed out, the more energy you will have to put into your race. You've already traveled and accommodated for the weather. You've ridden the course. And now you're one day out. It's important to start your race day preparations 1 to 2 days before the race. This chapter will give you guidelines on how and what to prepare the day before the race as far as your food and equipment followed by specific riding tips for race day, clues on how to stay motivated, the importance of knowing your opponents, guidelines for keeping up your speed, postrace cool downs and reviews, and finally examining the types of races and the racing schedules that are right for you.

RACE DAY-1

As race day looms there are many things to consider—food, drinks, clothing, equipment, and, of course, having time to manage it all. Being prepared is the key to performing well in any race. Not only do you have to be physically ready but you must be mentally ready and not worrying whether you packed enough sports drinks and peanut butter! The following sections will give you some guidelines on organizing yourself so that when it comes down to the day, you'll be prepped and ready to ride.

Packing Food and Drinks

If you do nothing else for 3 days before your race, make sure you drink a lot of water. The formula I use is that you should be making at least one trip to the bathroom during the night, the night or two before your race. If it is not happening, you are not drinking enough water. Our bodies are 55 to 70 percent water, depending on what source of information you use. With a 3 percent loss of fluid, your cycling performance will decrease by 3 to 7 percent. It may not seem to be a significant amount but it can be the deciding factor in a sprint finish or at least a 4-minute difference in a 2.5-hour race. Also, if you are consistently 1 or 2 minutes behind the riding buddy you have been dying to beat, try drinking a bit more fluid during the ride and you will be amazed how good you feel when you go screaming by them at the end of a ride. If you are not to fond of the tastelessness of water, add some lemon or other juice to your water bottle—whatever it takes for you to drink more.

Getting good nutrition before the race is also very important. If you are unsure of what you should be eating the day or two before your race and you want detailed information, talk to a registered dietitian who specializes in sport-related diet. What follows are some general guidelines on proper nutrition, including the recommended sources of calories, which are 60 percent from carbohydrates, 20 to 25 percent from fat, and 15 to 20 percent from protein. See table 12.1 for a sample menu for 1 week before the race.

Carbohydrates are still the most important energy source for cyclists, so make sure your plate is full of carbohydrates such as potatoes, rice, pasta, vegetables, and fruits. Fat is something we all need to keep our bodies functioning correctly. Do not worry about getting enough fat but make sure you are not cutting it out of your diet. If you are eating a well-rounded diet (following the percentages just noted), you should have some fat lurking in the area. Protein is helpful in repairing those

Table 12.1 Sample Prerace Day Menu

Day	Breakfast	Lunch	Dinner
Sunday	Poached/hard-boiled egg Whole grain tortilla Fresh salsa and avocado	Lentil soup Green salad	Herb roasted chicken Baked potato Steamed vegetables
Monday	Green smoothie with whey protein powder, flax seeds, and banana	Roasted chicken sandwich Green salad	Savory baked fish Quinoa Asian cabbage salad
Tuesday	Baked fish Whole grain tortilla Tomatoes and sour cream	Tofu stir fry	Roasted turkey breast Glazed yams Green salad
Wednesday	Green smoothie with whey protein powder, flax seeds, and banana	Roasted turkey sandwich Green salad	Chicken and rice Salsa and guacamole Whole grain tortilla
Thursday	Oatmeal w/cinnamon Fresh fruit, yogurt, nuts, and seeds	Veggie frittata Green salad	Zucchini pasta with Marinara sauce Baked tempeh
Friday	Scrambled eggs Whole grain tortilla Fresh salsa	Steamed vegetables Quinoa	Vegetable curry Green lentil dal Mango chutney
Saturday	Green smoothie with Whey protein powder, flax seeds, and banana	Veggie and hummus wrap	Teriyaki chicken Brown rice Asian greens

©Leigh Trombley

muscles you have stressed while training. I like to make sure all of the athletes I work with get some form of protein in every meal, especially at breakfast, where many athletes do not get enough. Some protein sources that are good for breakfast are eggs, beans, and cheese, which can be put in a breakfast burrito; nuts and seeds, which you can add to oatmeal; and soy or dairy milk, which you can add to cereal or add to protein powder to make a shake. If you are in a hurry, you can always grab a protein bar. Several tasty bars are on the market that have a good supply of protein.

Once you have found the best fuel for your engine, or what food your body runs best on, make it in to a routine. For instance, my prerace dinner was always salmon, rice, and broccoli or some form of green vegetable. It worked for me, so I stuck with it. It may be hard to get salmon in a small ski resort in Spain in the dead of summer, so be a little flexible or bring your own food.

One more word about eating–breakfast. Breakfast the day of the race is probably the hardest meal to get in to your system. If you tend to have a big case of prerace jitters, get a good drink mix that has carbohydrates, protein, and a little fat in it. If you are able to choke down some food the morning of the race, some old standards are: oatmeal with protein powder and peanut butter, a bagel and eggs with a little butter, a breakfast burrito with eggs and cheese, or even rice and beans with a little cheese. Having eaten well the day or two before the race, you should have sufficient fuel to help you during your race, so don't fret too much about the race day meal. Again, the key is to find what works for you and stick with it so that you don't have to think about it before your race. You will have enough on your mind.

Getting Organized

Make a habit of preparing your food and drink the night before the race, including what you will drink before, during, and after the race as well as any food you may want to eat immediately after your race. My typical drink preparation was four bottles of carbohydrate mix that would be consumed during the race, two bottles of what I called liquid food (a powdered drink mix that contains carbohydrates, protein and fat), and two bottles of water. Several of the energy drink producers such as Shaklee, Metabol, Endurox, and Accelerade have "liquid food" drink mixes that have all three energy sources in them. I consumed one serving of liquid food before the race and one after. I had one water bottle on the bike during the race and one in the feed zone in case I wanted it during the race. I would prepare all my bottles the evening before the race and put them in the refrigerator. I would also set out my gels, which are a good source of easily digestible carbohydrates, and bars for after the race. I sometimes even made a sandwich that I would bring to the race in a cooler so that I had something to eat afterward. To recover more quickly, it is important to get some carbohydrates with a little protein in your body within 30 minutes of finishing your race. So, don't think you are finished after your race is over; you still need to refuel your tank.

Equipment and Clothing

Make sure you check all of your equipment the night before the race. I don't mean rebuild your bike. You should have your bike in perfect running order at least two days before the race. Never change anything on your bike the night before the race if at all possible. It may come back to bite you during the race in the form of a flat tire or miss-shifting. You should, however, check the bolts and skewers on your bike to make sure they are all tight.

What I really mean by checking your equipment is to make sure you have all the tools you will need such as a tire iron and CO_2 cartridges or pump. Also, make sure your spare tube does not have a hole in it. In other words, pump it up and find out, especially if you have a spare tube in your saddlebag that has been in there for a month or two. The tube can get worn by rubbing on the saddlebag, which will create a weak spot or hole. You don't want to find these things out when you are on the course with a flat tire. I like to carry a multitool along with me. Several lightweight kinds are available. Make sure it has a chain tool and a few different sized Allen keys on it; broken chains do happen. If you are in the mountains of Steamboat Springs, Colorado, with no one in sight, it would be beneficial to fix your broken chain instead of hiking all the way back to the ski resort, 10 (O.K., maybe 7) miles down. Basically, your equipment checklist should be:

- Gels
- Tire iron
- Multitool
- Tube, partially pumped
- Check tube in saddlebag
- Chain tool

It's a good idea to set out your clothes the night before a race: jersey, shorts, socks, shoes, helmet, and anything you plan to wear for warming up such a windbreaker and leg warmers. I would rather not have to hunt for clothes the morning of the race when I should be out warming up. It is also important to set out your race number or even pin it on the night before. These tips are especially important if your race is at 7 a.m. the next morning.

And last but not least, sleep! Sleep is very important for having enough energy to race. With that said, most people do not sleep well the night before a race. If that is the case with you, don't stress about it; you are not alone. The most important night to get some good sleep is actually two nights before the race. Two nights before the race, you should not be as nervous and should be able to get a good, sound sleep.

TIME TO RIDE!

Race day is here, and the clock is ticking. Everything you do in the next few hours before you mount the bike is essential to your racing success. Have a good breakfast, look the part, warm up, know your focus, and hit the road! This section will give you tips on staying motivated, knowing your opponents, keeping up speed at the finish line, cooling down, and reviewing your ride after the race.

- Eat breakfast. We have already discussed what foods to eat for breakfast. The other aspect you want to get a handle on is when to eat before the race. The general rule is to eat 2 to 2½ hours before your race starts, which is no problem if your start time is 9:00 or 10:00 in the morning. If your race is at 7:00 or 8:00 a.m., you will either want to get up early or just have a drink mix that has carbohydrates and proteins in it up to 1 hour before your race. If your race is in the afternoon, you should eat a good breakfast and then have a snack or a drink mix 1½ hours before your race. Again, you have to experiment with what your body can tolerate but I would not put any solids in any later than 1½ hours before your race. They will most likely not digest and you will be a little sluggish during your race. Or worse, your body might decide to rid itself of the food altogether.

- Look the part. Do you ever notice other riders on the trail or at the start of a race? Which ones do you think look super fast without even watching them ride? It is most likely the riders whose bikes are sparkling clean and who have a perfectly matching kit or outfit. I remember lining up at the start of a race as a beginner (yes, I was a beginner at one point), and looking around at the other women. I would line up behind those racers who looked good because I thought they would be the fastest racers. I came to find out that looks weren't everything; money can buy you looks but not speed. However, the mental game is huge in any sport, and you should do anything you can to psych yourself up and make your opponents nervous. If you look good, you will exude confidence, which will give you the upper hand on your competitors at least at the start of a race. So clean that bike!

• Warm up. Along with having your equipment laid out before the race, you should also know what you will do for a warm-up and where you will perform it. I have seen and tried various warm-up routines. Many experts suggest riding a prescribed number of minutes at specific heart rates, which is best done on your trainer. If this routine works for you, stick with it. I found trying to keep track of minutes and heart rates the hour before the race to be tedious and stressful. I would also rather be riding on a road or trail instead of on a trainer.

The reason to do a warm-up is to get your body ready to race. In a mountain bike race, you have to be ready to go all out when the gun goes off. With that said, you need to make sure you have taken time to slowly get your muscles warmed up as well as perform some hard efforts so that your body isn't shocked when you blast off at the start line. I suggest the following warm-up:

1. 15 to 20 minutes easy or in zone 2 to 3

2. 3 or 4 × 3 minutes at or just above LT with 3-minute easy spin in between each interval; in other words, find a 3-minute hill and go up and down it 3 or 4 times at moderately hard pace.

3. 3 or 4 × 8, 15-second sprints with a 2-minute easy spin in between each interval; in other words, practice some starts from a rolling stop.

4. Another 10-minute easy spin to the start line.

This warm-up should take you between 45 minutes to an 1 hour to complete, so give yourself some time. If your race is a short circuit or time trial, make sure to get at least an hour-long warm-up. If you have a longer race that may not start off all out, your warm-up need not be as long.

When finding a place to warm up, you may want to think about riding to the course or looking at a section of road or trail that is near the start line. Most races take place out of the city, so you should see a safe road to warm up on. I choose to warm up on the road or trail because it tends to calm me down. If you do not find a good place to ride your bike, a trainer is a good option. It will allow you to be close to the start line and be able to get a specific warm-up routine done. As always, find what works best for you and stick with it.

• Know your focus. Once you're warmed up, it's time for the race and time to put all of your hard work to the test. As you line up, find something to focus on while standing on the start line so that your mind isn't wandering when the gun goes off. Be prepared. It doesn't mean that you can't do a little chatting with your fellow racers, but stay alert. When the countdown starts, you should be ready to go ballistic off the start line. Something I have tried to focus on is the line I will be taking. You have chosen or been placed at a certain spot on the start line, which will give you one or more options as to what line you can take. For instance, if I am called up and end up in the second row just behind Alison Dunlap and Mary Grigson, I know Alison is a fast starter and Mary comes on more at the end, so I may choose to get behind Alison when the gun goes off. On the other hand, Mary is sitting on the outside right and the first corner is to the left. I may choose to try and get all the way on the outside right to have the option of coming around Mary if she isn't going fast enough. When I am sitting on the start line, I pick a strategy and focus on where I will be going after the start. You can also think about what you will be doing in the first few minutes of the race, such as getting around any riders that are in front of you before the first single-track section. It doesn't hurt to visualize a good performance.

© Roving Photo

Focus, focus, focus! Get mentally psyched and train your mind on the finish line.

- Hit the trail peddling. Starts are one of the most important parts of a mountain bike race. If you plan to be finishing in the top 10, you better be in the top 15 within the first 10 minutes. Some racers can come from farther back and still place in the top 10, but they are few and far between. You will have not only a physical but also a mental advantage to being in the top 10 to 15, 10 minutes in to a race. If you are in the top 10 after 10 minutes, the pace will generally slow down a bit and you will be able to get into a rhythm. If you are not in the top 15, you will have to keep fighting for your position, which may mean trying to get past racers that are dogging it through the first single-track or technical section. You will be expending energy while the top 10 riders regroup.

Being in the top 5 to 10 within the first 10 minutes will also give you a mental advantage. The first time I found myself in the top 10 group of women in a race, I was so ecstatic I felt as though I was flying. This feeling of exhilaration will help make the race feel effortless and may fuel you to pick off a few more riders. Just think of how it would feel to be in the lead: It's like being superhuman and no one can touch you.

Being a good starter takes the physical strength, tactical ability, and mental wherewithal to know you can get where you need to be. Because the start of the race is very important to me, I have people diligently practice their starts, as in the specialization II phase discussed on page 160. Not only should you practice starts by yourself to get the physiologic effect, but it helps to practice different lines, different terrain, and clipping in and out of your pedals while on your own. It is also important to practice starts with a group of people to help you with your tactical skills. It will give you the ability to try different positions as if you were on a start line so you can get the feel for what it is like to try and get around other racers.

There is no way for me to educate you on all of the possible scenarios in a start; they are all different. Your best bet is to get as close to the front line as you can. If you are in the front line, you have a clear shot; just get in the best line on the course and hammer. If you are in the second or third row, pick the line you want to be in or the person you want to follow and get there as fast as possible. For example, if I am lined up in the third to fifth row, I try and get as close to the outside as possible and I assess who is around me that starts fast and who I need to get around. After the gun goes off, I thread my way through the racers as best I can. If I get stuck behind or in the middle of a group, I calmly wait until a gap opens up and go for it. In this situation, I might also look further up the course to see where the first climb is and wait until then to make my move.

Any time there is a slower rider in front of you who you want to go around, it is a good idea to tell them you are coming around and on what side so they are aware of you and don't decide to make any fast changes.

It is important to be aggressive but in a calm fashion. Being dangerously aggressive is a waste of your energy and can cause an accident that may put you 5 minutes behind the lead group. Generally, within the first 2 or 3 minutes after the start, riders begin to open up and gaps are created in the pack. Any time you are stuck or are lined up really far back, wait a few minutes and then go as hard as you can to get to the lead group. If you think you can do it, you will!

I will never forget watching Alison Sydor come around me in the start of the Vermont Nationals. I was lined up in the second row and she was in the 5th or 6th row. About 30 seconds after the starting gun went off, I was jockeying for 5th through 10th place and here comes Alison threading through two of us who were pretty close together. She was on a mission to get in to the top 3 and no one was going to stop her. I thought it was a bit dangerous, but she made it through without any of us crashing. I think she placed 3rd in that race.

I also remember lining up in the second row at the World Cup in Canmore, Canada, which was one of the Olympic qualifying races. I was right behind Chantel Decourt, who was a very good rider. When the gun went off, she couldn't get her shoe in her pedal and I was stuck behind her. It took me several seconds to get around her and by that time I was behind 20 racers. I knew a climb was coming up and waited until then to gun it. I was able to pass at least five people on the climb and ended up in 10th place overall in the race. I always wonder what would have happened if I had gotten a better start.

A handful of riders can come from 20th place to get into the top 5, so don't count them out. You may also be a slow starter who can pick up speed throughout the race. It is an energy boost to continue to pick off racers throughout a race, but the gap that the top 10 riders can get on the rest of the pack within the first 10 minutes is generally hard to make up.

Staying Motivated

The third and fourth laps of a five-lap course were the most grueling for me. At this point the racers are fairly spread out and you may not have another racer in sight. This situation is truly where the mental game comes into play. If you are thinking, *I am starting to get tired and I still have to climb that hill two more times*, you are going to be in big trouble. Of course, it may pop into your head but you should try and change that story as soon as possible or you will start to lose energy and slow down. A better way to stay energized is to focus on what is in your immediate future. I don't mean that beer you will drink after the race; I mean that if a fun technical section is coming up, think about how you are going to rip down it. If a long climb is coming up in the next 5 minutes, think about how you will power up it. Tackle what is directly in front of you with enthusiasm. Otherwise, you will be overwhelmed and lose steam. Don't worry, this mental game goes back and forth for most of us. Just make sure you steer it in the right direction when you find yourself thinking negative thoughts.

You can also use some visualization in the middle of the race to help motivate you. Most of the time, spectators are on the course either rooting for you or for one of your opponents. Often they will be giving you splits, which means they will be telling you how far you are behind the racers directly in front of you. It can motivate you to pick up the pace to try and catch them or you can visualize yourself closing the gap, which will help you to pick up the pace. In my case, it works better if I know someone is close behind me. In that case, I visualize one of my opponents closing the gap behind me, which motivates me to pick up speed. When I start to lose motivation, I also think about smoothing out my pedal stroke. If nothing else, it gives you something to do while you wait for the last lap to come around.

It is very important to keep the water and gel flowing. In the first third of the race, you need to start drinking carbohydrates, and because you have looked at where you want to drink when preriding, you know where those sections are. To stay strong at the finish, you need to keep pounding the liquids through the middle third as well and possibly do a gel. Sometimes a caffeinated gel in the middle of a race is just the ticket to get you fired up to catch the person ahead of you.

Knowing Your Opponents

The more you race, the more you will get to know who you are racing with. Try to learn these attributes about your opponents: Do they start fast? Are they good climbers? Can they descend well? Are they the type to come from behind to pass you toward the end? Knowing these things about your competitors will help you to determine where you should be in relation to them during a race. For example, if you know that Alison is a fast starter, it would not be a bad idea to line up behind her at the start. I knew that Mary Grigson was one of those racers who could be in 15th place halfway through the race and still get into the top 5 before the race was over. In that case, if she was behind me coming up on the last lap, I knew I couldn't let up or she may come around. It is very crucial to know whether the racer in front of you is a good descender when coming up on a single-track descent. If they do well, you can be sure and follow their line. If they are more tentative, you better get around them before the single track or you will be losing time.

Keeping the Speed

Being able to keep your speed up in a race lasting more than 2 hours is a skill that every racer needs to work on. You may be the type of racer who can ride for long distances but have little speed. In that case, you may want to take up ultra distance racing or work on intensity. But if you can go fast for 1½ hours before you start to slow down, you better work on your endurance as well as hydration and nutrition. The ability to keep the hammer down toward the end of the race is important because it would be better to have a gap on the person behind you than to have to sprint—unless you are a good sprinter.

A sprint finish is not something that happens often in a cross-country mountain bike race; however, you should be prepared for anything. As I have mentioned in the section on preriding the course (see page 175), you should be aware of what the course does leading up to the finish

Keep the speed and be prepared to sprint to the finish.

line. If you are doing several laps of a course, you can get a feel for the finish while racing. If you are doing five laps of the course, on the third or fourth time through the start and finish area, practice sprinting. It will give you an idea of where you need to be for the last lap, if in fact you are close to other racers.

If it looks as if the race may come down to a sprint, you should be aware of where the last corner is in relation to the finish line, what way the corner turns, and the best line to be in coming out of the corner. If you are riding close to someone you know is a faster sprinter than you are, you better make a move to get ahead of them before the sprint. Also, make sure you are in a fairly hard or big gear before the corner because once you come out of the corner, you will need to stand up and gun it.

Cooling Down

A good cool-down is a key part of recovering from a hard race. Cooling down means continuing to ride at an easy pace for 20 to 30 minutes after your race is over. Part of the cooling-down process should also include getting some food into your body. Mountain bike racers tend to congregate at the finish line and talk about their race. That is fine to do, but make sure it is only for a few minutes. Better yet, convince some of the other racers into cooling down while talking over your race. The reason you want to make sure to cool down after a race is to slowly bring your heart rate down. It is not good for your body to go from an all-out pace to a complete stop. It will also help to clear the lactic acid from your muscles and help to keep your muscles from cramping. For the best recovery, make sure to do an easy, 20- to 30-minute spin directly after your race.

While you are cooling down, have something to eat or drink. Many racers have a hard time digesting solid foods directly after a race. If this is the case for you, you should find a liquid meal replacement drink that you like and use it. I have a bottle filled with a meal replacement drink that I pick up after the race and force myself to drink while I am cooling down. It is important to eat something within ½ hour of the end of your race because this is when your body will take up the most nutrients. Find what your body can tolerate and make it part of your after-race routine.

Reviewing Your Ride

In order to learn from each race, it is a good idea to go over what happened during the race with someone who is willing to listen. It can mean talking to a friend or family member who understands and is able to be subjective about what happened during the race. Better yet, review the race with your coach or sport psychologist because they will have a good understanding of who you are and how you have done in past races. Some of the topics to discuss are what you did well during the race and what you felt you could work on for the next race. No matter whether you came in first place or dead last, you can find at least three things you did well and three areas you need to work on. For example, one race that comes to mind is a National event in Mammoth, California, in 1999. We lined up at the start and I was on the outside of the first corner: "On you mark, get set, go" and we were off. Bombing up the hill and starting around the first right-hand turn I got stuck on Shonny's bar ends and she yanked and I went down. Then Sheri Cain proceeded to ride right over me—thanks, Sheri. After the dust cleared, I got up and found my bars and stem were tweaked to the side. I tried physically moving them but they wouldn't budge. I got out my multitool, loosened the stem, realigned the bars, and got going again. By this time I was only about 5 minutes off the last rider. I rode the first half lap with my visor hanging off my helmet before I ripped it off. By that time I was in cruise mode and just wanted to finish the race. After the first full lap I had picked off 10 to 12 riders. The next lap I picked off another 10 to 12 and by the last lap I was gunning for the top 10. I ended the race in eighth place with a smile on my face and a whole new outlook.

When I talked with my sport psychologist about that race, we discussed what I had learned. First off, I would change whom I lined up next to on the start line and what line I chose to take on the first corner. I would also plan to go a bit harder off the starting line to avoid the crowd. I learned that if you are in the front line, taking the inside or middle of the corner may be fine as long as you are in the lead. What I did well was not give up and keep a good attitude throughout the race. I also discovered that I could come from behind and make up a lot of time on the pack if I just stayed calm and went at my own pace. This experience was obviously a positive one, which will generally leave you feeling good about your race. I have had more than my share of bad races that have left me feeling worthless as well.

If you race at all, you will have a bad race. You may start off and have difficulty getting clipped in to your pedal, causing you to lose time. You may feel sluggish and unable to get enough energy to keep up with your usual group or you may crash or have a mechanical problem that puts you behind. We are all unhappy with our race results for many reasons. Again, my suggestion is to find a willing ear and talk about your race. You will find that a difficult race is more of a learning experience than a race you did well. These races will make you a better racer as long as you realize what went wrong and make changes. What you will also find is that you did some things well in those races, and you should also talk about those aspects. For example, I remember racing in the World Cup race in Vail, Colorado, in 1997. I ended up flatting at least twice during the race; I was not happy. I think we discovered that my rim had a rough spot or my rim strip was bad. I learned to make sure these were both checked before every race. The positives were that I was able to fix a flat in a short amount of time and again, I could make up time in between each flat. I also had a good start and was able to keep a good position before the flats started happening.

It is also important not to wallow in misery after a bad race. In the beginning of my racing career, I would kick myself for several days after a bad race. I felt I was not good enough and would never be able to ride with the fast girls, and so on. It is okay to get a little down on yourself—it is only natural—but don't let it go on for several days or a week; it's a huge waste of energy. Allow yourself a day or two of negative thoughts but then move on. Instead of getting down on yourself, use that energy to fuel your training. Get mad and make changes in your training and racing so you will be flying by the next race.

RACING WHAT'S RIGHT FOR YOU

How much racing can you tolerate before you are cooked? And is racing a good training tool? It is important to find what works for each individual, and not look at what Alison Dunlap or Jeff Kabush are doing. When you first take up racing, it is a good idea to slowly increase the number of races you attend. Many people also like to race into shape or use racing as their training. I believe racing is a very good way to help increase your fitness level and get your race routine down, but it has its limits. This section will discuss how to progress the number of race days and ways of using racing as a training tool.

The first year of racing is basically an experiment. Pick out a few races in your area and just have fun with them. Don't put any pressure on yourself to have results. Having some top finishes is great, but if you don't that is fine as well. You are just learning the process, meeting new people, and hopefully going to some cool places.

After each year of racing, you should slowly increase the number of races you do. Racing is obviously very stressful, not just because of the physical aspect of racing, but from packing and unpacking your bike and equipment, staying in hotels or camping out, not sleeping in your own bed, and traveling and eating different foods as well as the stress of being nervous about your event. All of these things can take a toll on your body. Similar to slowly increasing the time or intensity on your bike, you should slowly increase the amount of racing you do. It will give your body time to adapt. For example, if during the first year of racing you compete in 5 races, the next year do 7 or 8. Don't just jump ahead and do 12 major races. You may think you can tolerate doing a lot more racing, but I have known several people who have burned out and quit racing altogether because they increased their racing too rapidly. If you increase your races too rapidly, you are also more likely to get an overuse injury, such as tendonitis or bursitis, which can take weeks or months to heal.

Different levels of racing exist. For example, the local evening race series will be much less stressful than going to a regional or national event. So take this fact into consideration when looking at increasing your racing. You should be able to do more local racing with less stress to your body than if you were to do more national events. For example, your racing time line should look something like table 12.2.

Table 12.2 Racing Timeline

Number of years racing	Local or evening races	State races	National races	World Cup races	Number of total races
< 1	5	2	0	0	5-7
1-2	5	5	0	0	7-10
2-3	5	5	2	0	10-12
3-4	For training	7	2-3	0	12-15
4-5	For training	5-7	3-5	1	15-20
5-6	For training	For training	All in the series	1-3	20+

Be aware that this table is one example of how to increase your races and the difficulty of races each year. Everyone is different and will progress at different rates. You may only want or be able to do the state series races and therefore you will continue to race at that level. You may want to work up the ranks in your state series from beginner, to sport, expert, and maybe pro, instead of going to higher-level races. You may have come from a different sporting background and progress at a more rapid pace. Use table 12.2 as an outline to give you an idea of how to progress.

After you have raced for a year or two, you can start looking at races as a way of training. Some people say they are racing into shape, which means many of their hard workouts are actually races. The only true way to know how fit you are is to enter a race. In that way, the first race of your season should be a training race and not a peak race. You may be surprised at how hard it is and how much more training you need to do to be ready to really race.

It is also a good idea to use the local races or evening series races as training. Or, if you are new to racing, this is the best way to get your racing skills down in a less intimidating setting. It is a great way to ensure a high-intensity workout or work on your technical and tactical skill without being too stressed about your finish. You need to be aware, however, that if you are the type that kicks yourself when you don't do well, using races as training may not be a good idea. Your mental well-being may outweigh the benefits of getting a hard workout and just doing a hard group training ride may be a better way to go.

Road and stage racing make great training tools but it's also important to know when you've reached your peak and enough is enough.

- Race to train. Road racing can be a very good way to increase your fitness for mountain bike racing. Road racing is less taxing on your body and can be less stressful if it is not your true sport. Road races can usually be found in your local area as well and therefore you should not have to travel too far to race. Again, these are a way of pushing yourself a little harder than you would if you were riding on your own.

Stage races are also an excellent way of training for mountain bike racing. A stage race can be either a road or mountain bike race that lasts anywhere from 3-7 days. O.K. the Tour de France is a 21-day stage race, but I highly doubt anyone would be using that race for training. I like to use a stage race as a training camp. You should have no other obligations such as work or family during that time so you can strictly focus on getting some high-intensity workouts while being able to eat well and rest. For example, in 2000 I did the Redlands stage race as well as the Tour of Willamette in Oregon. During these races I would get up, eat a good breakfast, and then go out and race hard for several hours. When I got back I would eat again, sleep, get a massage if I was lucky, eat again, and sleep. This way you are sure to get several days in a row of hard training with good recovery in between. You will be amazed at how strong you are for mountain bike racing 2 or 3 weeks after a stage race. Be sure to schedule the stage race appropriately in your training scheme and take a rest week afterward. It will take you a few weeks to realize the strength that you have gained.

- Reach your peak. A racer can realistically peak two or three times in one year. When you first begin racing, your results will most likely be all over the board. One race you will be in the top 5 or 10, the next race you may be off the back. This is because your body has not adjusted to the time and intensity of racing. After you have a few years of racing in your legs, your body will have adapted to the demands of racing and you should be able to more closely predict how you will do in a race. The first few years will look something like a bell-shaped curve, with one peak in the middle where you feel your best. After several years of racing, you should see more of a wave type curve in your racing model, with one to two peaks where you felt your best and the lows not dipping down quite so far. After 7 to 10 years of racing, you should have honed your skills and adjusted your training in a way that your curve looks more like a flat line with 2 or 3 blips in it where you will be peaking. In this scenario you still have those peak races, but the valleys are not so dramatic and you remain fit enough to place in the top 5. This is the ultimate goal of a good training program but takes 5 to 10 years, so be patient.

- Know when to say when. If you feel as if you are cooked, you probably are. Learn to listen to your body and take a break when you need one. If you are on a team that requires you to race a certain series or number of races, you may not have a say in the matter. In that case you should either talk with the manager of the team to see whether you can take a race off, or be sure to take a week or two of easy training in between your races. If you are on your own schedule and you feel yourself getting burned out, take a race off. If you continue racing at this point, the rest of your season will most likely be mediocre. Once you take a weekend or two off of racing, you will be refreshed and ready to rock. The hardest part is listening to your body and knowing the signs of burnout or overtraining. The best way is to keep a training log or journal and watch for the symptoms of overtraining as mentioned in chapter 10 on page 167.

Never lose focus on what part racing plays in your life. You may think it is the only thing that matters. If that is the case, you will be in for some serious letdowns. I loved racing and wouldn't have changed my years of racing, but during my race season I would have to take a reality check every few weeks. Up until my last year of racing, I worked as a home health physical therapist to help pay for my racing addiction. The job was perfect because it allowed me to schedule my patients around my training time. I definitely had days when I got off the bike, ate, went to see patients, and almost passed out because I was dehydrated or didn't have enough food. But, overall it was the perfect job. The work really helped me to realize that racing was just a small portion of my life. I would go to the homes of people who had had strokes, head injuries, heart problems, or a number of different illnesses, and they where having difficulty getting out of bed. After working with these people, I realized I was lucky to even be able to get on my bike and ride, let alone race. Don't lose sight of the big picture. Every race you finish is a huge accomplishment; don't belittle where you end up. Lastly, realize racing and riding is truly a luxury, so enjoy it to the fullest.

BIBLIOGRAPHY

Burke, E. R. 2002. *Serious cycling.* Champaign, IL: Human Kinetics.

Fry, A.C., and Kramer, W.C. *Sports Medicine.* 23 (1997): 106-129.

Girard, S., with USA Cycling. *Training manual for mountain biking.* Colorado Springs, CO: USA Cycling, Inc., 1998.

Hamley, E.J. Physiological and postural factors in the calibration of the bicycle ergometer. *J. Physiology.* Jul: 191 (2): 55-56. 1967.

Holmes, J. C., A. Pruitt, and N. Whalen. Lower Extremity Overuse in Bicycling. *Sports Medicine.* Vol. 13. No. 1, January 1994.

Jeukendrup, A. E. 2002. *High-performance cycling.* Champaign, IL: Human Kinetics.

Trombley, Leigh. N.C. Certified nutritionist (415) 721-0839.

LeMond, G., and K. Gordis. 1987. *Greg LeMond's complete book of bicycling.* New York: G.P. Putnam & Sons.

Pruitt, A. L., with F. Matheny. 2002. *Andy Pruitt's medical guide for cyclists.* Chapel Hill, NC: RBR Publishing Co.

Randall, W. "Elite Coaching." Lecture given on Nov. 16, 2001. US Olympic Committee, Expert Level Coaching Seminar, Colorado Springs, CO.

USA Cycling. 1995. *Expert coaching manual.* Colorado Springs: USA Cycling, Inc.

INDEX

Note: The italicized *f* and *t* following page numbers refer to figures and numbers, respectively.

A

aluminum frames 6

B

Ballantyne, Sarah 177
Barnholt, Kerry 61, 64
bars 20, 29
Bergeron, Jergen 115
bike fits. *See also* bars
    crank arm length 18-19, 19*t*
    description of 14
    frame size 14-15
    full suspension, hard or soft
        tail bikes 13-14
    physical variables 21-22
    saddle height 15-16, 16*f*
    saddle position 19, 20, 20*f*
    stem length and height 17, 18*f*
bike shoes, fitting 22
brakes 10
Brown, Travis 87, 123
Burke, Edmund 106

C

Cain, Sheri 175, 197
carving turns. *See also*
        countersteering and
        braking in corners;
        cornering in challenging
        conditions
    key elements in 43
    pedal placement 44, 45*f*
    setting up and execution 48
    technique 47

    weight shifting technique 43,
        43*f*, 44
climbing
    decreasing body weight 27
    energy conservation 35-40, 37*f*
    increasing watts or power
        output 27
    pedaling uphill 29-35
    redistributing body weight 28,
        28*f*
    repositioning bike for lower
        center of gravity 28, 29
cornering in challenging
        conditions
    cornering skills 50-52, 50*f*, 53*f*
    gravel and sandy conditions 49
    loose-sweeping fire road
        corners 49
    switchbacks 52, 53*f*
    tight cornering conditions 49
    tips for improving 53-54
    wet or muddy conditions 49
countersteering and braking in
        corners
    braking 45, 48
    countersteering, description of
        45, 46*f*
    skidding 48
Craig, Adam 94

D

dismount, run, and remount
    carrying bike on back 117, 118*f*
    cyclo-cross race 115

ABOUT THE AUTHOR

Ann Trombley works as an elite cycling coach to participants of all ages, abilities, and disciplines. She has been a mountain biker for 20 years and has competed for 10, during which time she earned a spot on the U.S. mountain bike racing team at the 2000 Sydney Olympics, won the National Short Track Championship, and placed 12th at the World Championships.

© Courtesy of Rob Karman

Trombley received a bachelor of science degree in movement education from the Dominican College and a master's degree in physical therapy from the University of Colorado Health Sciences Center. She is currently a physical therapist at the Boulder Center for Sports Medicine in Colorado. She also runs women's mountain bike clinics, which are designed to help women improve riding skills, assess bike fit, and learn basic maintenance skills. Trombley has been a member of the board for the National Off-Road Bicycling Association (NORBA) and USA Cycling.

Trombley resides in Boulder, Colorado, where she cycles, gardens, and camps in her spare time.

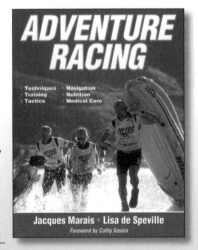